NOTTING HILL & HOLLAND PARK PAST

First published 1993
by Historical Publications Ltd
32 Ellington Street, London N7 8PL
(Telephone 071-607 1628)

ISBN 0 948667 18 4

Typeset by Historical Publications Ltd
and Fakenham Photosetting

Printed in Hong Kong by the
South China Printing Company

NOTTING HILL&
HOLLAND PARK
PAST

A Visual History

by
Barbara Denny

HISTORICAL PUBLICATIONS

TO PHILIP DENNY

Acknowledgements

My debt to those who have helped me in the preparation of this book goes back many years to the late Mr C. G. Boxall, the post-war Reference Librarian at Kensington Public Library and a great authority on the history of the locality. In more recent times his work was continued by Mr Brian Curle, in charge of the Local History Collection, who has produced a number of informative articles and papers on the area. Research on this book and the selection of many pictures was greatly assisted by Carolyn Starren, the present Local History Librarian at the Local Studies Centre in Kensington Central Library.

Liz Bartlett of the Kensington and Chelsea Community History Group has provided much information both on the past of the area and the changes which have taken place since the construction of Westway and the setting up of the Notting Hill Amenity Trust.

The Notting Dale Urban Studies Centre gave me permission to use pictures from their interesting past publications such as *Our Homes - Our Streets*.

Last but not least I should like to thank my publisher and editor, John Richardson, and my husband, Philip Denny, for his support and encouragement.

Further Reading

The Survey of London, Vol. XXXVII: Northern Kensington (1973).
Barton, Nicholas, *The Lost Rivers of London* (1962, new edition 1992).
Bowack, John, *Antiquities of Middlesex* (1705).
Cathcart Borer, Mary, *Two Villages* (1973).
Campden Hill's Historic Houses and Their Inhabitants (Kensington & Chelsea Libraries)
Evans, Geoffrey, *Kensington* (1975).
Faulkner, Thomas, *History and Antiquities of Kensington* (1820).
Gaunt, William, *Kensington* (1975).
Gladstone, Florence, *Notting Hill in Bygone Days* (1922).
Gladstone, Florence, *Aubrey House, Kensington, (1698-1920)* (1922).
Hudson, Derek, *Holland House in Kensington* (1967).
Ilchester, The Earl of, *Chronicles of Holland House* (1937).
Ilchester, The Earl of, *Home of the Hollands, 1605-1820* (1937).
Hunt, Leigh, *The Old Court Suburb* (1855).
Ferguson, Rachel, *We Were Not Amused* (1958).
Ferguson, Rachel, *Royal Borough* (1950).
Ferguson, Rachel, *Passionate Kensington* (1939).
Jenkins, Simon, *Landlords to London* (1975).
Kennedy, Ludovic, *10 Rillington Place* (1961).
Kensington News 1869-1972 (files).
Kensington News Centenary Supplement (1969).
Kensington Gazette 1853-55.
Kensington Society *Annual Reports* 1954-1992.
Lefebure, Molly, *Murder with a Difference* (1959).
Ridgeway, Brig. G.R. *Past Notabilities of Kensington* (1935).
Ridgeway, Brig. G.R., *A Short History of Campden Hill Square* (1932).
Rosen and Zuckerman, *Mews of London* (1982).
Whelpton, Eric and Barbara, *The Intimate Charm of Kensington* (1948).

The Illustrations

The following have kindly given their permission to reproduce illustrations:
The Royal Borough of Kensington and Chelsea: bookjacket, frontispiece, 1, 8, 9, 10, 12, 14, 17, 18, 19, 21, 22, 37, 38, 45, 53, 55, 58, 59, 70, 72, 73, 74, 75, 78, 88, 92, 104, 105, 113, 114, 118, 122, 123, 124, 128, 130, 139, 157, 165, 167, 172
The Greater London Record Office: 57, 95, 107, 110, 135, 166
Notting Dale Urban Studies Centre: 102, 103, 106, 117, 119, 120
David Ingham: 173
All other illustrations were supplied by the Author or the Publisher

The bookjacket is an oil, probably painted by William Mulready's son, of Notting Hill Farm in 1745.

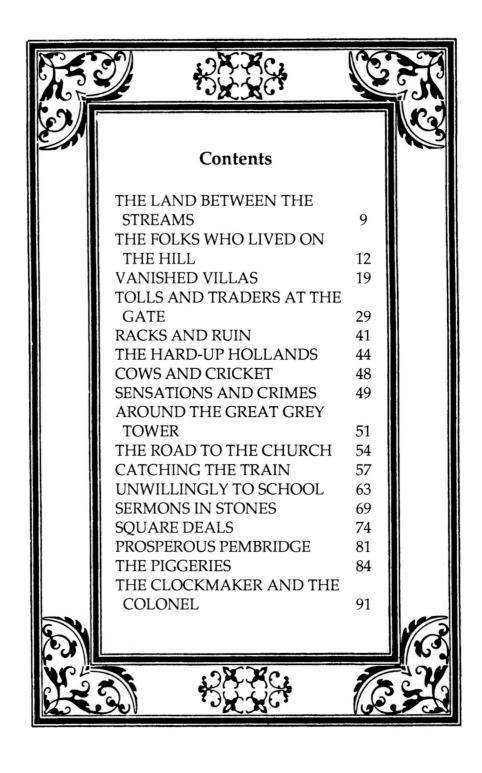

Contents

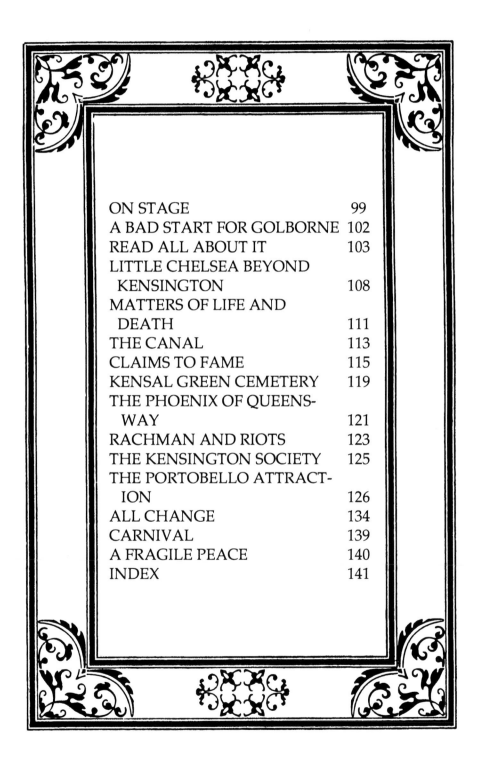

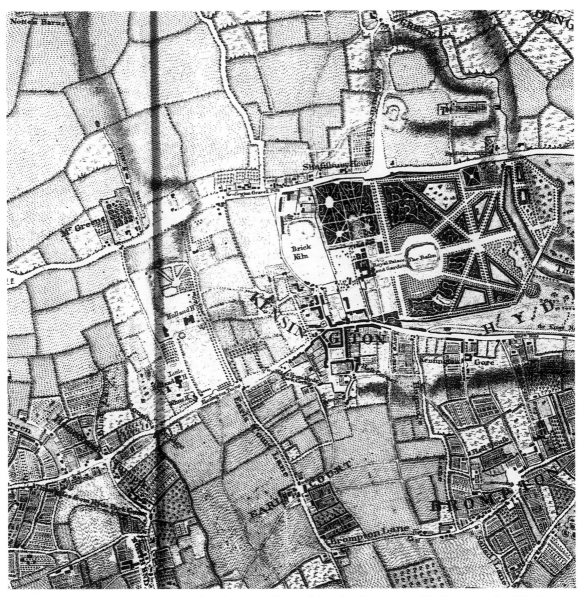

Part of John Rocque's map of the Environs of London, c1745. The parallel roads today represented by Kensington Road/Kensington High Street and Bayswater Road/Notting Hill Gate/Holland Park Avenue, are in the centre of the map, north and south of Kensington Palace and Kensington Church Street. Notting Hill Gate is called \ Kensington Gravel Pits, and there is a large brickfieldand kiln to the east of Church Street. Holland House is shown to the west.

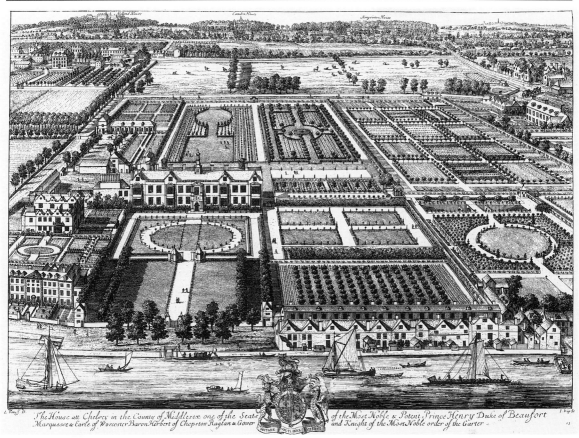

1. *'The house att Chelsey', aerial view of c1680 looking north from Beaufort House in Chelsea in the foreground to Kensington. On the three hills in the distance are Holland House to the west, Campden House in the centre, and what became Kensington Palace to the east of them.*

The Land between the Streams

In the summer of 1605, the second year of the reign of James I, a passenger on a barge drifting slowly upstream on the Thames towards the marshes of Chelsea, could look towards low hills on the northern horizon, still thickly wooded as they had been since Roman times. It was an entirely rural aspect, but hidden among trees, just beyond the little village of Kensington - merely then a church and a cluster of cottages - the builders were busy on a mansion for one of the king's favourites, Sir Walter Cope 'of the Strand'. He was then one of the richest men in the land, a property dealer, entrepreneur and money-lender, and the house he built was large enough to be called 'Cope's Castle', the first of several handsome dwellings in the vicinity. This early influx of the rich

and famous and the later move of the court of William and Mary to Kensington, gave the area its 'royal' cachet. The story of Notting Hill and Holland Park as suburbs of London dates from the time of their arrival.

But, to begin earlier. In Roman times, when the roads from Londinium were formed, a main route was that of Bayswater Road and Holland Park Avenue, which led to Silchester. Another road is believed to have existed parallel to it, on the line of modern Kensington High Street and Hammersmith Road, leading to the northern route at Acton. Supporting evidence for the Bayswater Road line was printed in an edition of the *Gentleman's Magazine* in 1841. It was noted that during the building of the Ladbroke Estate, a stone coffin containing an adult skeleton was found six feet below the turf by the road, with remains of other wooden coffins nearby, as well as bone and ivory pins. The burial of the dead within the precincts of Roman towns was forbidden and it was the custom to inter them along roadsides.

The area that was to become the Royal Borough of

Kensington (before its amalgamation with Chelsea) was bounded on the east and west by two streams, the Westbourne and Counter's, or Billing's, Creek, respectively. These waterways, rising in the hills to the north of London - Counter's Creek at Kensal Rise and the Westbourne at Hampstead - meandered down to meet the Thames at Chelsea.

To the north, Kensington's boundary with Willesden lay along a 'crooked horse track' connecting Paddington to Harlesden (the Harrow Road). In the south the old Fulham Road divided Kensington from Chelsea. The Thames, a much wider and shallower river than it is today, flowed through low marshy land (when Thomas Cubitt developed Belgravia he had to raise it above the flood level by transporting soil up river from the excavations for St Katharine's Docks). Just north of Kensington village, however, the ground rose slowly to 100 feet above sea level up to the ridge which is now Holland Park Avenue and St John's Hill.

It is thought that around 700AD a party of Saxon immigrants, the 'sons of Cynesige', attracted by the high wooded ground, established a 'tun' - a simple stockaded community - on the lower slopes of this hill amid the vast forest of Middlesex to give birth to 'Cheniston' or Kensington, while others of the same tribe, the Cnotingas, or sons of Cnotta, settled a little further up the rise. This prosaic explanation of the

two place names is preferred now to the more romantic association with nut trees which Notting Hill enjoyed for many years.

William the Conqueror gave the manor of 'Chenisintun', roughly the area of the borough of Kensington (except that it did not include the territory west of Ladbroke Grove), to Geoffrey, Bishop of Coutances, under whom Aubrey de Vere, a member of an important Norman family, was chief tenant - the de Veres were later to be Earls of Oxford.

By the 12th century the estate was sudivided into four quasi-manors - Earl's Court, West Town (between Kensington High Street and Holland Park Avenue, west of Holland Walk), Notting Barns (north of Notting Hill Gate) and the small Abbot's manor of about 250 acres between the present Church Street and Addison Road. The Abbot's manor was given by de Vere to the Abbot of Abingdon as a reward for care of his sick son, and in so doing he laid the foundations for the dedication of St Mary Abbot's church and for several street names.

The de Veres forfeited the northern part of their estate, the Notting Barns manor, in 1462 when the 12th Earl of Oxford and his son, Aubrey, were executed by Edward IV for their Lancastrian allegiance during the Wars of the Roses. The 13th Earl, long in exile, eventually regained his inheritance by supporting Henry Tudor - he fought alongside him at the

2. *'The Royal Palace of Kingsington', a hand-coloured print of Kensington Palace sold during the 1690s.*

3. William Cecil, Lord Burghley. Oil painting by an unknown artist.

Battle of Bosworth Field in 1485. But he was so impoverished that he had to sell the estate in 1488, to William, Marquis of Berkeley, the Great Marshal of England, from whom it once again passed to the Crown when he sold it to the king's mother, the scholarly and pious Margaret, Countess of Richmond and Derby. At this time the manor was valued at £10 per annum and consisted of 'a messuage, 400 acres of land fit for cultivation, 5 acres of meadowland and 140 acres of woods'. On her death the Countess bequeathed the estate to the Abbot, Prior and Convent of Westminster, specifying that the income should be used for Masses to be sung for the repose of her soul at Westminster Abbey, and for the upkeep of endowments she had founded at Oxford and Cambridge universities.

By now, pasture and hayfields had supplanted the old woodlands. The 'Knotting Barns' manor was let by Westminster Abbey to a City goldsmith and alderman, Robert Fenrother, and it formed the dowry of his eldest daughter on her marriage in 1518 to a gentleman sheep farmer, Henry White.

The young couple preferred not to live in the manor farm house which stood in the midst of arable land, meadows and woods where St Quintin Avenue joins Pangbourne Avenue, but in a house a considerable distance away, called Westbourne Place, near Royal Oak. Both Henry and his wife died in 1535 (possibly of plague), leaving five children for whom

the estate was put in trust. In the same year, with the Dissolution of the Monasteries, freehold ownership reverted to the Crown, although Robert White, the oldest of the children, was allowed to remain temporarily in the family home before being obliged to exchange his tenancy for land at Southampton.

Subsequent tenants of Notting Barns Manor included William Cecil, Lord Burghley, and it was on his death in 1598 that it was sold to Sir Walter Cope for £2,000. Cope had already bought West Town (around the area of Addison Road) in 1591, and later on he acquired Earl's Court as well. Notting Barns was probably a speculation on his part, for two years later he sold it on at a good profit to Sir Henry Anderson, a City of London alderman, whose family eventually became the manor's freeholders.

The boundary between the northern part of Kensington and Paddington meanders uncertainly between Bayswater and Harrow Roads, indeterminate enough for residents to claim that they live in Bayswater rather than in the less prestigious Paddington. The name of Bayswater derives from Baynard's Watering, a place on the Bayswater Road where water was customarily drawn from the river Westbourne. South-west of Hampstead this stream passes under the Kilburn High Road, the Grand Junction Canal and Paddington Station, and then emerges in Hyde Park where it feeds the Serpentine.

Paddington remained almost entirely rural until the early 19th century, with no grand mansions to attract a settlement of servants and tradesmen. Instead, its proximity to London made it a convenient larder for London's milk, vegetables and fruit. Unlike Kensington, it remained, except for a short period, in ecclesiastical hands and in 1816 the Church of England began its development, under the guidance of the architect, Samuel Pepys Cockerell, who himself resided in an elegant house at Westbourne Place, the same site which had been the home of the White family some three hundred years earlier. Even today, a large part of Paddington and Bayswater is owned by the Church Commissioners.

Most curious of all in the history of these local communities, is that of Kensal New Town, the most northern part of Kensington. This wooded area had become part of Chelsea in the 11th century as a result of a bequest; by the time the Whites came to live at Westbourne Park in c1518 it consisted of four fields which Henry White leased for agriculture. Although still part of the manor and, later, the parish of Chelsea, this detached land became Crown property until Mary Tudor sold it to one of her physicians. The local administration of the area continued in the hands of Chelsea parish until 1900, when the numerous London parishes were organised into boroughs. At that time Kensal New Town was given back to a reluctant and ungrateful Kensington.

The Folks who lived on the Hill

COPE'S CASTLE AND HOLLAND HOUSE

When Sir Walter Cope bought the freehold of Abbot's Manor in 1599, he acquired with it a stubborn sitting tenant, Robert Horseman, who was reluctant to leave. Indeed, there was a long-standing feud beween the two men. A compromise was reached whereby Cope took possession of a part of the estate on which to build a house, while Horseman retained his home near the old church, called The Parsonage, and 200 acres, which included the area of Campden Hill as well as land north of 'the road to Uxbridge' on the Norlands estate.

Horseman died in 1600 before Cope had begun to build what became Holland House, and in 1616 his son sold the house and about 70 acres to Sir Baptist Hicks, another wealthy royal favourite, who had already become a neighbour by buying a 'capital messuage and two closes known as the Racks and Kings Mead' from the Crown in 1609; it was on this newly-acquired land that Hicks built his own grand mansion that was to rival 'Cope's Castle'.

Cope's house, known famously as Holland House, deserves more space than is possible here, for it had a social role in London for three centuries., What follows and on p44 is a brief outline of its history.

Although additional wings were added twenty years later, the house, possibly designed by John Thorpe, began as an already extravagant mansion, matched only by the lavishness of the entertainments provided for the owner's guests. A visitor in 1609 writes in a letter of a 'solemn dinner' he had just attended there. 'Besides good cheer and the fair show of the house newly trict and trimmed for the purpose we had a Morris Dance and the King's Cormorants to entertain us', the latter being birds used to catch fish for the guests from the stocked ponds, their throats bound so that they could not swallow them.

Cope was not to have long in his new home and he was planning improvements and additions in 1614 (though heavily in debt) when he died, leaving the house and land to his wife and thereafter to his daughter, Isobel, who came into possession when her mother remarried. Isobel made a good marriage to Henry Rich, Earl of Holland in Lincolnshire and Baron Kensington, and second son of the Earl of Warwick; he was everything that people perceived a good nobleman to be - tall, good-looking and wealthy. What is more, he was willing to continue with the improvements to the building, then known as Kensington House. His failing, however, was indecisiveness, demonstrated in the Civil War when he switched sides either out of uncertainty or expediency, and eventually finished on the losing side. As a result, Rich's handsome head, defiantly wearing a smart lace cap, was severed from his body at Westminster on 9 March, 1649.

The house was then taken over by Cromwellian

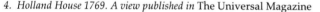

4. Holland House 1769. A view published in The Universal Magazine

5. *The grand staircase at Holland House as it appeared in the mid-19th century when the house was in its glory, lavishly furnished and containing a magnificent library. The last great social occasion was a ball in July 1939 attended by George VI and Queen Elizabeth, a few weeks before the outbreak of war.*

forces as headquarters for Colonel Fairfax, but Henry Rich's widow was soon allowed to return: her social life resumed, and her building improvements continued. Her son, who eventually inherited the house and the Warwick earldom, died in 1701, and his widow married Joseph Addison, essayist, poet and Secretary of State. By 1746 the house was taken by Henry Fox, who bought the freehold in 1768 a few years after he had become Baron Holland.

Fox had a long and turbulent political life in the Whig interest, which culminated in his being appointed Paymaster General, a post from which he derived an enormous fortune, so large that even in those corrupt days the scale of his peculations was raised and he was accused by the City of London of being 'the public defaulter of unaccounted millions'. His son, Charles James Fox, became a famous politician and, like his father, a reckless gambler.

Later occupants were the third Baron Holland and his wife, Elizabeth. She, at 23, had already had

6. *Holland House in ruins, c1950.*

five children by her marriage to Sir Geoffrey Webster, but so captivated was she by the young Lord Holland that she obtained a divorce from Webster in 1797, while expecting Holland's child. Despite the scandal (or perhaps because of it) she became one of the leading hostesses of the day and Holland House was a hub of literary and political life, which embraced a strong partisanship for Napoleon Bonaparte. Elizabeth, too, took an interest in the development of the house and its grounds - it is thought that she was responsible for the first importation of dahlias into England.

Holland House continued as a centre of society throughout the life of the 4th Lord Holland, though he suffered poor health. When he died in 1859, childless, his wife gave up residence at Kensington, although she returned for short periods of lavish entertainment.

Her general extravagance and its resulting financial embarrasment caused her in 1873 to make over the house to a distant relative, Lord Ilchester, who was already her heir, in return for an annuity. The house remained in the occupancy of the Earls of Ilchester for over eighty years. On the night of 27/28 September 1940, during the London blitz, it was hit by incendiary bombs and disastrously damaged. For a period, when peace returned, there was much talk of the house being demolished altogether and the grounds built upon, but it was sold to the LCC in 1952, and after a vigorous campaign by the newly-formed Kensington Society, the east wing was restored for use as the King George VI Memorial Youth Hostel, together with new buildings designed by Hugh Casson and Neville Conder, and the extensive grounds were opened as a public park.

The Orangery remains intact and is used for art

mansion, with turrets surmounted by cupolas, bays with large windows, and an ornamental porch. It was approached from the main Kensington road by a long avenue of elms. The formal gardens which surrounded it are today bounded by Sheffield Terrace, Hornton Street, Gloucester Walk and Kensington Church Street.

Hicks died in 1629. In his will he left £200 'to be yearly employed for the good and benefit of the poor of the town of Kensington'. This founded the Campden Charities, supplemented later by a further £200 from the Viscountess Campden, and £150 from Oliver Cromwell. The Viscountess's bequest also included a sum to 'put forth money for one or more poor boys of the parish to be apprenticed.' The resources of Campden Charities have since grown to many millions of pounds and are used for purposes well beyond the intentions of the 'very harsh man' who made the bequest.

Baptist Hicks' descendants retained the house until 1708, when it was sold and used as a boarding school for girls. In 1691 it had been let to Princess (later Queen) Anne and Prince George of Denmark, while they searched for a house in which to bring up their delicate small son, Prince William Henry; Little Campden House was built in the grounds to accommodate the Princess's suite.

Campden House returned to private occupation in 1847, when its occupants included a Mr William Frederick Wolley, who built a theatre there in which Charles Dickens acted in *The Lighthouse* in 1854. But then disaster struck - the house was burnt down in 1862, and although a replica (perhaps even more ornate) house took its place, this had a short life and was demolished in 1900. The site was used to build Campden House Court flats. As for Little Campden House, it was first divided into two dwellings, was badly damaged by a bomb in 1944, and then demolished to build the Tor Gardens LCC estate.

BEGINNINGS OF KENSINGTON PALACE
Another wealthy man was building a large house at the same time as Cope and Hicks. Sir George Coppin, Clerk of the Crown to James I, bought 36 acres from Hicks on the border of his Kensington estate with Westminster, and commissioned the same architect as used by Cope - possibly John Thorpe - to build what became Nottingham House, named after a later owner, Sir Heneage Finch, speaker of the House of Commons, who was created first Earl of Nottingham in 1681. This building provided the nucleus for Kensington Palace when William III and Mary chose it as their London home in 1689.

Thus, three large houses were built in the fields of Kensington, but it was to be another hundred years before the rural charm of the area was disturbed and they were joined by others.

exhibitions and concerts; the tiny Ice House, used to provide ice for the lavish banquets of the past era, now houses small art shows; in the grounds the Dutch Garden and other features, reminders of the whims of previous occupiers of the house, still survive.

THE CAMPDEN HOUSES
As we have seen, part of the Cope freehold land was taken by Sir Baptist Hicks, a man made wealthy in the early part of the 17th century by money lending, and one 'who knew how to amass money as a merchant and spend it as a prince'. His own residence, Campden House, thought to have been built in 1612, might well have been an enlarged development of an earlier timber-framed building. In any event, Hicks, who became a Viscount, taking his title from his seat at Campden in Gloucestershire, erected a fine Jacobean

7. *Holland House 1898, lithograph by T.R. Way*

8. *Campden House c1647.*

9. *Campden House c1860, south-east view from the flower garden. Coloured lithograph by Edwin Smith.*

10.   *Amateur theatricals at Campden House. Scene from the play* The Lighthouse. *From an 1855 woodcut.*

11. *Little Campden House, built c1690 to accommodate Princess (later Queen) Anne's suite when she and Prince George of Denmark were renting Campden House.*

12. *Thorpe Lodge, Campden Hill, from the garden*

Vanished Villas

A VAIN CAMPAIGN

Only Thorpe Lodge, one-time home of a Governor of the Bank of England, Montagu Norman, survives out of nine elegant and interesting houses which could be considered the minor mansions of Campden Hill. The Lodge is now part of Holland Park School and as such escaped the appalling destruction of these fine buildings. In 1949 the Campden Hill Preservation Society was formed for what proved to be a largely vain attempt to save the older mansions that were left and more modest villas of more recent date. The Society also aimed to prevent the erection of flats in the area. The Society was accused of elitism and snobbery, but the protesters said that they were opposed not only to LCC flats in the area, but to *any* flats at all. In propitiation, Lord and Lady Norman offered the garden of Thorpe Lodge as a public open space, but as they held this only on lease the offer had no great promise. Not many flats did materialise after the Public Enquiry, but nevertheless the old mansions fell.

Thorpe Lodge was one of seven houses on Campden Hill produced by John Tasker, an architect eminent in the early 19th century. Norman took it in 1904 and added greatly to its decor and furnishings. When the LCC announced its development plans in 1948 there was a particular outcry about the Lodge and though it was saved from destruction it was lost as a residence. The music room, which Montagu Norman had created from a studio on the west side, and which was once used by the Victorian artist, Henry Tanworth Wells, became the school library.

Elm Lodge was not so lucky, being the first of Tasker's houses to go as early as 1878 to build Airlie Gardens. In common with much other property in the vicinity, the freehold had been bought by the Grand Junction Waterworks Company, which anticipated the construction of their new reservoir there in 1843; for a time the house was occupied by their engineer.

Bedford Lodge, now recalled by Duchess of Bedford's Walk, with its modern luxury flats, was the home of the Duke and Duchess of Bedford from 1823 (the Dowager continued to live there until 1853). This was one of the Hill's most elegant houses. The Duchess's drawing room was decorated with white and gold panelling brought from a French château, and the Victorian painter, Sir Edwin Landseer, advised her on the layout of the gardens. After she died the house was taken by the Duke and Duchess of Argyll,

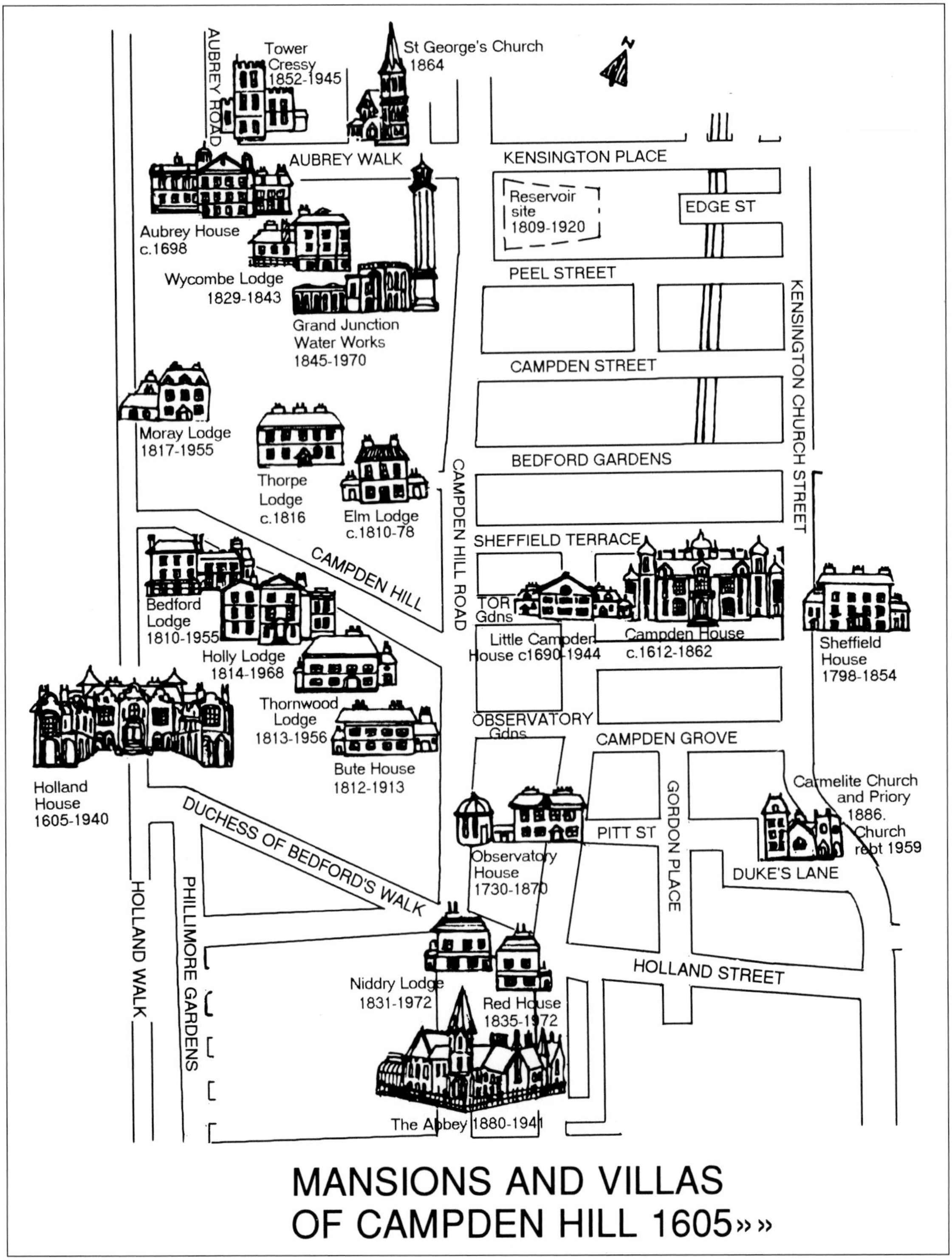

AUBREY ROAD

Tower Cressy 1852-1945

St George's Church 1864

AUBREY WALK

KENSINGTON PLACE

Reservoir site 1809-1920

EDGE ST

Aubrey House c.1698

PEEL STREET

Wycombe Lodge 1829-1843

Grand Junction Water Works 1845-1970

CAMPDEN STREET

KENSINGTON CHURCH STREET

Moray Lodge 1817-1955

Thorpe Lodge c.1816

Elm Lodge c.1810-78

BEDFORD GARDENS

CAMPDEN HILL

CAMPDEN HILL ROAD

SHEFFIELD TERRACE

TOR Gdns

Little Campden House c1690-1944

Campden House c.1612-1862

Sheffield House 1798-1854

Bedford Lodge 1810-1955

Holly Lodge 1814-1968

Thornwood Lodge 1813-1956

Bute House 1812-1913

OBSERVATORY Gdns

CAMPDEN GROVE

Holland House 1605-1940

DUCHESS OF BEDFORD'S WALK

Observatory House 1730-1870

PITT ST

GORDON PLACE

Carmelite Church and Priory 1886. Church rebt 1959

DUKE'S LANE

HOLLAND WALK

PHILLIMORE GARDENS

Niddry Lodge 1831-1972

Red House 1835-1972

HOLLAND STREET

The Abbey 1880-1941

MANSIONS AND VILLAS
OF CAMPDEN HILL 1605»»

13. *Mansions and Villas of Campden Hill area 1605 onwards. Map by the author.*

and named after them. The Duke was an enthusiastic ornithologist and spent much of his time studying the variety of birds which frequented the grounds.

The ground landlord, Sir Walter Phillimore, lived in the house after the Duke's death; his estate stretched down to Kensington High Street (Phillimore Gardens is a reminder). After his death in 1929 the house (renamed Cam House after Phillimore's property in Gloucestershire), was leased to a wealthy American, Mrs St George, who left her own mark on the villa. A huge work force was employed for three months for alterations which included the erection of new entrance gates, topped with fish-shaped lanterns, and the inclusion of the old door from Newgate Prison, set up where the garden wall flanked Holland Walk. In addition, the figures of St George and the Dragon were erected on the frontage and Plane Tree House was built in the garden. Both houses were requisitioned by the Army during the Second World War, and both were demolished to make way for Holland Park School.

BUTE AND MACAULAY

The site of Bute House is now largely covered by the Queen Elizabeth College. It is believed to have been the earliest of John Tasker's houses. In 1812 its first resident was Richard Gillow, probably a member of the cabinet-making firm, Waring & Gillow, but the name of the house commemorates a later occupant (1830-42), the Marquess of Bute. The University of London took a 999-year lease of the site in 1914, after the house had been demolished, for its King's College Women's Department. The College (now renamed after Queen Elizabeth II) also swallowed up neighbouring Thornwood Lodge in 1956. Built in 1813, this house had had as residents the surgeon-apothecary, Thomas Kitching and Sir John Fowler, railway engineer.

All that is left of Holly Lodge, formerly the residence of the historian, Lord Macaulay, is the modernised coach house. Macaulay spent his last years here, moving from his previous home in Albany, Piccadilly, in 1856. He took great delight in the large garden with its lawns and rhododendrons. In a letter to a niece, he wrote "I have no friends near me but my books and my flowers and no enemies but those

14. Bute House, Campden Hill

execrable dandelions! I thought I was rid of the villains but when I got up the day before yesterday and looked out of the window I could see five or six of their great impudent flaring faces turned up at me! How I enjoyed their destruction! Is it Christianlike to hate a dandelion so savagely?" Revived in health in the rural peace of Kensington after the bustle of London he was hard at work all through 1856/57 on the fifth volume of his great *History of England*. "I feel as if I had just begun to understand how to write; and the probability is that I have very nearly done writing," he wrote to a friend. The words were prophetic. By 14 December 1859 the *History* was finished, but on 28 December Lord Macaulay was dead, seated in his library with an open book beside him.

In 1968 the house was demolished for a further extension to Queen Elizabeth College.

15. *Thomas Babington Macaulay, from a painting by Sir Francis Grant*

16. *Holly Lodge, Campden Hill, Macaulay's home*

17. The Red House, Hornton Street; view from the garden. Watercolour by M. Conway, 1904.

THE MORAY MINSTRELS

Moray Lodge, the most westerly of the houses, with a boundary on Holland Walk, was demolished in 1955 to build Holland Park School, having also been requisitioned during the war. In the mid 19th century, during its occupation by Arthur Lewis, a wealthy silk merchant, it was a centre of artistic and social events. Lewis, founder of the Arts Club, married the actress, Kate Terry, and the oldest of their four daughters became the mother of John Gielgud. Lewis assembled around him some of the brightest artistic talent of the day to join in The Moray Minstrels, who met at the Lodge for 'billiards, singing and to go to Bohemia for a night'. These included William Makepeace Thackeray, Charles Dickens, John Millais, Arthur Sullivan and George du Maurier, and it was here that *Box and Cox* was produced for the first time, with du Maurier as Bouncer.

Public indignation did not save two other houses, although they survived until 1972, when the new Town Hall was erected. Niddry Lodge and the Red House were situated on the north of the Town Hall site and the latter was utilised for a time as Council offices. Niddry took its name from its second occupant, in the 1840s, the Dowager Countess of Hopetown whose husband, the fifth Earl, was also

Baron Niddry. This house had been built by Stephen Bird, a well-known brickmaker and builder, and a few years later he built himself a house next door, the Red House, Hornton Street. Bird played a prominent part in the construction of drains and sewers in Kensington and Westminster. Later occupants of the Red House included Herbert Hoover, who became President of the United States. In his memoirs he described his London home as 'a house with a quaint garden in the middle of a great city' and 'as a place of many happy memories and many stimulating discussions.'

The War, not development, destroyed The Abbey, an ornate Gothic folly, also on the Town Hall site, which reflected in its architecture and its name the eccentric humour of its first owner, William Abbot. It was built of Kentish ragstone with carved embellishments; the interior was equally ornate, with a Great Hall, Grand Staircase, panelling, statues, and stained glass windows depicting Arthurian legends. It was left extensively damaged after bombing and the site was eventually used to build the new Town Hall and Public Library in Hornton Street.

18. *Hornton Street 1889, looking south from the junction with Observatory Gardens. Watercolour by E.A. Gladstone.*

A SPA IN KENSINGTON

Aubrey House, to the north of Campden Hill remains virtually unchanged from its appearance a hundred years ago. It was built in 1698 by Dr John Wright, a 'doctor of Physick', John Stone, an apothecary, and two others, to use as a spa, utilising the waters of a medieval well which had been discovered among the nearby gravel pits. Dr Benjamin Allen's *Natural History of the Chalybeat and Purging Waters of England*, published in 1699, contained an analysis of the alkaline water which was said to be 'mildly purgative, containing Epsom or Glauber Salts', and was doubtless beneficial to those who over indulged at their dining tables.

This was a period when mineral water spas were very much in fashion. John Bowack, writing in his *Antiquities of Middlesex* in 1705, described Kensington as a 'handsome populous place, especially in the Summer months when it is extremely filled with lodgers for the pleasures of airy walks and gardens around it...and a famous Chalybial Spring.'

The Well's fame was shortlived, however, and by 1720 the spa house had become a private residence, that of Edward Lloyd, later Secretary of State for War, when it was known as Notting Hill House. Then its extensive garden was even larger than today, and covered an area now occupied by Aubrey Road and Campden Hill Square. In 1767, by then called Aubrey House, it was taken by the eccentric Lady Mary Coke, nicknamed 'the White Cat', owing to her albino colouring and a penchant for gossip. A prolific letterwriter and journal keeper, she wrote of her times in an intimate and homely way with frequent catty details, sending 'chapters' regularly to one or other of her sisters. She was a wealthy widow

at 27, and her friendship with the Duke of York, brother of George III, gave her a status which she enjoyed even after his death as she expanded her life into a semblance of royal widowhood. Her early journals are full of Court gossip and politics, and display her range of eccentric grudges, obsessions and persecution complexes.

She had just turned forty when she came to Notting Hill. The property then included a flower and kitchen garden and an orchard, with a farmyard on the slope between the footpath that is now Holland Walk, and an avenue of lime trees (Aubrey Road). Artificial hills were then much in vogue and Lady Mary had one built in her garden so that she could sit and watch the traffic passing by on what is now Holland Park Avenue.

In addition to her spicey comments on the social scene, Lady Mary left interesting records of contemporary life at Notting Hill, the weather, her garden and her livestock. Flooding was quite frequent as streams built up in wet weather, especially in the autumn of 1768 when she saw 'two rivers, the grounds two or three miles off being all under water'.

Her garden was her delight and she notes mornings spent tying up honeysuckles, sowing annuals and weeding and planting a hundered 'perannual' [sic] flowers. The picture she draws is of seclusion: 'all here is in a state of silence so that it seems a

19. Lady Mary Coke, from a portrait by Allan Ramsay 1762.

20. Aubrey House c1830, originally the Wells House, where Lady Mary Coke lived for many years.

21. *The nursery at Aubrey House 1817. From a watercolour by Mrs L. Goldsmid.*

22. *The music room at Aubrey House, 1817. From a watercolour by Mrs L. Goldsmid.*

23. *The old Coach House, all that survives of Holly Lodge.*

deserted country' and the only drama was when her cow, 'Miss Pelham', strayed into another herd or the hunt rode through her grounds, much to her annoyance. Later, she leased a small plot of ground from the Hollands on which to build a cottage which became part of No. 7 Aubrey Road. She left the villa in 1788 and died, aged 85, in 1811, at the Manor House at Chiswick, leaving behind her a number of decrepit pets and a lot of rubbish.

Aubrey House was let to tenants after her departure, one of whom ran a school there. In 1873 it was bought by William Cleverley Alexander, a banker, and it remained in his family until the death of the last of his daughters in 1972.

Tolls and Traders at the Gate

A TURNPIKE ROAD

The main road through Notting Hill, 'the way to Uxbridge', had gravel pits on either side. In fact, the description 'near Kensington Gravel Pits' was used to describe the whole of northern Kensington as far as Kensal Green. The cluster of houses at Notting Hill shown on John Rocque's map of c1745 (see p8) is so small that it hardly merits the description of a village, and a set of etchings published about this time shows a rural scene of cattle meandering along a pretty country lane. The density of population had hardly changed when Thomas Faulkner published a map in 1829 and it is remarkable that in the space of barely thirty years afterwards development took place which changed the Notting Hill High Street, now named Notting Hill Gate and Holland Park Avenue, into a busy shopping thoroughfare, with a hinterland of the terraces of the Ladbroke and Norland estates. And, to the west of them, were the notorious Potteries, a deplorable, overcrowded slum.

The 'Gate' at Notting Hill originates from an Act of Parliament which authorised the collection of tolls along the Bayswater Road-Holland Park Avenue route, so as to pay for its maintenance. A Turnpike Trust was established which met at the George Inn, Acton, four times a year; toll gates and toll houses were erected, lamps placed at dark parts of the road and 'fit and able bodied men' were appointed to patrol the way to prevent robberies and murders.

25. From 'A Great Plan of the Great Road from Tybourne to Uxbridge' surveyed by Leddiard, 1769.

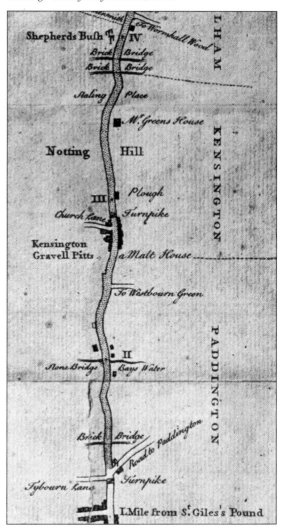

24. The road to Uxbridge from Britannia *by John Ogilvy, 1675*

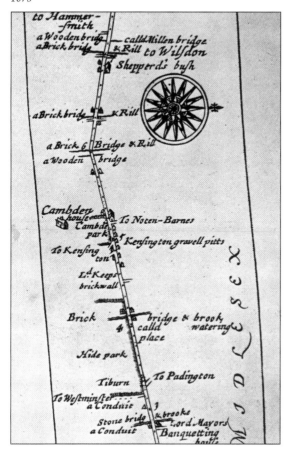

26. Sketch map of the principal features of Notting Hill Gate in the 19th century. Drawn by the Author.

The Kensington Gravel Pits toll gate was the first to be set up by the Trust in the mid-18th century, situated approximately at the present junction of the high street with Pembridge Road. Exemption from tolls was granted to citizens travelling to and from church, and no tolls were exacted on the day of an election.

The toll system in England was unpopular from the start, partly because the Trusts generally failed to carry out their obligations of repair and maintenance, and were suspected of pocketing too much of the toll money. By 1854, the newly-established *Kensington Gazette* was vigorously campaigning for the abolition of the Notting Hill gate, supported by correspondents. Gates had apparently already been removed from Hyde Park Corner and King's Road, Chelsea, and a letter from 'J.G.' in 1855 remarks that 'The extension of London is looking to the west, its more rapid progress is impeded by the tolls'. These he describes as 'an obstruction to intercourse between the gentry and the traders'. 'I regard the keeper of the tollgate as a legalised highwayman, he

lays hold of your bridle, pats your horse and puts on the stance of a regular brigand telling you to stand and deliver!'

Another correspondent supports this view, saying that the presence of the toll gate was driving the gentry from the area and their houses were being converted into shops; it had cost him two tolls of fourpence halfpenny to travel from Queens Road, Bayswater to Gloucester Place, Kensington. 'The Russian knout is preferable to such an affliction'.

A few weeks after this letter the toll-keeper, Henry Woodward, was ordered by the magistrate to return a threepenny toll and pay two shillings costs to a man who had wanted to pass with a cart laden with 'fat black soil' (earth and manure), for which he claimed exemption, it being for agricultural use.

Reinforcing the toll gate, bars were erected across adjacent side roads, such as Church Street, Pembridge Road, Addison and Norland Roads, so as to prevent circumnavigation, though this measure became increasingly impractical as development spread.

27. Notting Hill tollgate 1835. This was the second of three gates erected in the High Street between the mid-18th and 19th centuries. It stood at the junction with the lane to Portobello Farm (now Pembridge Road).

28. *Kensington Gravel Pits. These were situated on the south side of Bayswater Road, including part of what is now Kensington Gardens, and in patches scattered on the north side. In 1672 a document complained that excessive digging of gravel had encroached on the ancient rights of the church owners of the manor and their tenants. Painting by John Linnell, c1811.*

29. *Notting Hill Toll Gate, looking west. From a watercolour by Paul Sandby, 1793.*

30. *The last tollhouse at Notting Hill, removed amid much rejoicing in 1864.*

All the bars and gates were removed in 1864, an occasion of great rejoicing, with cavalcades of carriages and coaches passing through when the gates were opened at midnight on 1 July.

STORMONT HOUSE

In his *Old and New London*, the Victorian historian, Edward Walford, dismisses Notting Hill Gate as a 'roadway with small shops on either side, narrow and unattractive'. About the only residence of consequence must have been Stormont House, built in 1786 by John Silvester Dawson, who leased two acres of the Gravel Pits Estate from the Campden Charities (which are said to have acquired them with the gift they had received from Oliver Cromwell). Dawson's lease ran for 81 years at £38 per annum. The elegant house which he built, with large reception rooms and a 'square staircase', stood well back from the roadway behind a pair of ornate gates. In 1808 the house became a girls' boarding school run by a Miss Martha Tracy. By the 1850s it was being used by the Working Men's Association for evening classes. One advertised in the *Kensington Gazette* offers a lecture by a Mr Cable, 'a working man', on electricity 'with experiments, admission twopence.'

Although Stormont House remained, the land to its rear, which had been the site of the short-lived Trewson Brewery, had become covered with seventy small slum houses, known as Anderson and Pitts Cottages, built in the early years of the 19th century and which soon had the sobriquet of 'little Hell', being in 'a filthy condition, multi-occupied with a

31. Some 18th Century Buildings in Notting Hill Gate. Drawings by Miss E. Woolmer, c1924.

score of pigs in the back yards'. It was probably for the benefit of the children living in these that in 1860 two charitable ladies, Miss Desborough and Lady Gray, began a Ragged School in Stormont House. In 1867, when the lease of the land fell in, the whole area was redeveloped and the site of Stormont House became No. 1 Clanricarde Gardens, one of a terrace of 51 houses.

NEW FRONTAGES

Coincidentally with this development the northern frontage of Notting Hill High Street, with its tiny shops and narrow pavements, was replaced by a sedate terrace, which still survives, though updated. Facing this were the kitchen gardens of Kensington Palace, concealed from the public by a high red brick wall. A row of Queen Anne houses and some pretty cottages filled the space between the Palace gardens and the Mall.

The Victorian custom of developing roads as a series of separately-named terraces is well demonstrated by the complexity of addresses between the Mall and Campden Hill Road and Ladbroke Terrace. There was Greyhound Row, for example, between the Mall and Church Street, built on the site of the Gravel Pits almshouses which had been erected in 1711 and demolished in 1821. The shops here in the mid-19th century included Mr Brewer, grocer, cheesemonger and corn chandler, and a butcher called Price. This last shop, near the corner of Church Street, was later to become one of Notting Hill Gate's largest and most successful businesses, Shorts, which

survived until the 1960s as a grocer, butcher and provision merchant. When its founder, John Short, came to see the premises with a view to buying them in 1858, he said he found their present owner asleep on the doorstep with his pipe in his mouth.

When the *Kensington Gazette* was first published, an advertisement for a sea trip in aid of the Notting Hill Philanthropic Society gives an idea of the shopping facilities then available at the 'Gate'. The sponsors of this outing included a hatter, printer, bootmaker, the keeper of the post office, a plumber, fishmonger and many more. The excursion, to the Nore and Sheerness, was on board *The Petrel*, leaving from Waterloo Pier at 9am on 30 July 1855. The passengers would be offered the privilege of going over the splendid guard ship, *The Waterloo*, 120 guns, lying in the Medway. An excellent band would be on board 'for quadrilles and other dancing'. Tickets were priced at five shillings double to raise funds for the Society 'which had relieved 5872 persons with soup, bread and grocery during the previous inclement weather.'

32. Notting Hill Gate 1857.

33. Notting Hill Gate, 1857.

TRANSITION TO A SHOPPING CENTRE

The transition of Notting Hill Gate to a shopping centre was undoubtedly helped by the extension of the Metropolitan Railway's Circle line from Westminster to Edgware Road in 1868. Evidence for this may be gleaned from editions of the *Kensington News* in 1869, in which the mundane providers were augmented by Fortescue's, the hatters, a china emporium, selling a '108 piece dinner service' for £1.16s, a picture-frame manufacturer, a French and English dyer, numerous stationers and drapers, a bedding merchant and a tea merchant, F.W. Fricker, selling a huge variety of blends. Other traders included Mr Burden, a rag and bottle merchant, who is described as a 'great man on Kensington Vestry', renowned for his oratory, as well as being a proprietor of omnibuses. His wife, who kept a nearby greengrocery, was hugely fat so that when she died her coffin had to be lowered from the bedroom window.

The first shop to be lit by gas was King's Italian Warehouse, which stood opposite the entrance to Church Street. Near this, a late 18th-century double-fronted house was the home of Madame Vestris, the actress and singer, the first woman to become a theatre manager, and her husband, the actor, Charles James Mathews. Their house later became for a while an Institution for Teaching the Blind. On the site of

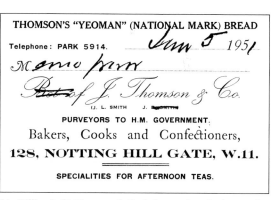

THOMSON'S "YEOMAN" (NATIONAL MARK) BREAD

Telephone: PARK 5914. *Jun 5* 195*1*

Memo from

Bot of J. Thomson & Co.

(J. L. SMITH   J. SMITH)

PURVEYORS TO H.M. GOVERNMENT.

Bakers, Cooks and Confectioners,

128, NOTTING HILL GATE, W.11.

SPECIALITIES FOR AFTERNOON TEAS.

34. Billhead of J. Thomson & Co, bakers and confectioners of 128 Notting Hill Gate, in 1951.

the old Central London Railway station on the corner of Pembridge Road was once a farm, its house surrounded by gardens and orchards, part of which later became the site of the Devonshire Arms.

When Mr R.T. Swain, auctioneer and estate agent, came to live at the corner of Campden Hill Road in 1848, his house, the elegant Lodge, had a large garden and orchard, but no mains water - his supplies were fetched from the public pump near the toll gate, where there was also a pound for stray cattle, and a

35. Notting Hill Gate from Kensington Church Street, by W. Cleverley Alexander,1912.

36. Notting Hill Gate in 1905.

forge. In 1869 Swain, who founded a business that was to endure for over a century, was advertising 'To let, a comfortable residence of nine bedrooms, dressing and sitting rooms, garden opening on to pleasant ground, £50 per annum.'

THE DISAPPEARING INNS

As a staging post on the way to the west, Notting Hill Gate had a large number of inns and taverns. All were at some stage rebuilt, but most are no more, or else have had their names changed, such as the Swan on the corner of Church Street, which is now the Rat and Parrot, and is in any case lost in a modern concrete block. Once it was a homely inn with a horse trough, and then a Victorian gin palace, all lights and glitter. The Hoop happily survives both in name and substance, though completely modernised. The Coach and Horses, which began as a primitive tavern on the north side of the high street, was first rebuilt in 1863 and by 1870 had become a station for coaches to Hayes and Hillingdon, and for omnibuses to Hanwell. Its Victorian splendour included huge hanging lanterns, which matched the ornate cupola of the Coronet Theatre opposite; the Coach and Horses was demolished in the 1960s' transformation and the 18-storey Campden Hill Towers is on the site. Similarly, the Plough, on the corner of Ladbroke Terrace, which once had an attractive tea garden at the rear, went at the same time. Happily, two flower-bedecked pubs in traditional style remain in the hinterland, the Uxbridge and the Hillgate Arms, in their respective streets, and the Windsor Castle has an attractive setting on the corner of Peel Street and Campden Hill Road.

37. The Three Horseshoes, near Kensington Gravel Pits. After R.H. Laurie, 1795.

38. *Unloading barrels of Charrington beer at the Windsor Castle on Campden Hill, early this century.*

39. *The old Mitre pub in Holland Park Avenue advertised 'good accommodation for cyclists' when they were still the kings of the road at the turn of the century.*

Racks and Ruin

As development took place along the high streets of Kensington and Notting Hill Gate between 1820 and 1840, speculative builders were looking seriously at the land between the two roads, to the east of the Holland Park estate. William Phillimore had already capitalised on his family inheritance between Kensington High Street and the villas on Campden Hill, and by 1820 several of the streets which still bear his name were lined with attractive terraces.

Higher up the hill, beyond the gardens of Moray, Thorpe and Elm Lodges, an area known as the 'Racks' had also been part of the Phillimore estate until it was sold in 1808. This 25 acres was split into smaller lots and changed hands several times before a young speculative builder, William Hall, bought five acres in 1822. Still not aged 21 when he signed the contract, he was already building in St Marylebone. Aiming high, he decided to develop his new land on a grander scale than that envisaged by other purchasers of the estate lots, who were a partnership of two other St Marylebone builders called Punter and Ward. Whereas Hall concentrated on one grand avenue (Bedford Gardens) of semi-detached villas with large gardens, the neighbouring builders cut their plot of approximately the same size into two, to create

Campden and Peel Streets, with much smaller houses aimed at a lower income group.

Despite serious financial problems, Hall and his family were able to complete about half their project before changes in ownership in 1831, and although this altered the character of the later houses their high class remained: 'substantiality and elegance is combined with an infinity of good taste'. They had four bedrooms, elegant reception rooms, a library, wine cellars and attractive large walled gardens with plenty of fruit trees - all this for £50 per annum, 'although a time is fast arriving when a considerable addition will willingly be given.'

Part of the north side of Bedford Gardens, near Church Street, had to be demolished in 1860 when the railway was built, and on the south side some of the plots sold by auction in 1823 remained empty for years and changed hands many times, before being redeveloped in a variety of styles that do not match the rest of the road.

The residents of such a development as Bedford Gardens could well support the volume of new traders at the 'Gate', but this could not be said for those in the houses of Peel and Campden Streets. Here, buildings were being erected piecemeal. On the south side of Campden Street, some of the plots had been even further reduced to provide larger gardens for the Bedford Gardens villas. Sewers were not constructed until many years after the first devel-

40. Campden Street c1900 long before it was transformed into 'desirable residences'. A baker's cart stands at the roadside.

41 and 42. Two late-Victorian views of Peel Street. In 1856 nearly all the houses were in multi-occupation - pigs were said to be kept there in a filthy condition and there were 'foul and offensive privies'.

opment and even in 1856 the Vestry was told that pigs were being kept in a filthy condition in one house, and that there were foul and offensive privies in several others.

Starling's map of 1822 shows the northern part of the Racks as a brickfield. These acres had been bought in 1810 by a wealthy Devonshire quarryman who leased it for brickmaking, although some speculative building was encouraged. It was not until 1851 that any concentrated development took place and when it did it was of the least prestigious kind, in what are now Uxbridge Street, Newcombe Street, Farm Place, and Callcott, Hillgate, Farmer and Jameson Streets. Over 200 houses went up in less than ten years divided over a number of small builders, and the freeholds were rapidly sold at a low price to landlords who saw them as investments. One, Edward Baker, paid £8,200 for over 100 houses. The 1861 Census reveals that most of the houses were multi-occupied - some accommodating over twenty people. One, in Jameson Street, had no less than 37 occupants in six families. Although Henry Mayhew, author of *London Labour and the London Poor*, reported that the occupants were 'pleased to be living in the suburbs', another contemporary writer considered Hillgate Street to be a 'dingy ill-favoured slum', and the vicar of St George's, Campden Hill, claimed that the conditions of these impoverished parishioners were no better than those in the East End.

Most of the houses on the east of Jameson Street and the west of Newcombe Street had to be taken down to build the new railway station in 1868. The latter has now been completely rebuilt since 1960, although the design of the new houses closely resembles the original on-the-street terrace without front gardens.

When the modern Notting Hill Gate redevelopment took place, old shops on the corner of Kensington Place and Church Street were demolished, but one or two of the villagey shops in Uxbridge Street, including a rag and bone and scrap metal merchant, survived into the late 1970s.

One of the last shops to go must have been the bakers, Wittekind's, on the corner of Uxbridge and Farmer Streets. Founded by Adam and Teresa Wittekind, who came to England from Germany in Victorian times, it remained in the same family ownership, although baking on the premises ceased some time in the 1960s in the face of public health regulations, and despite supportive protests and petitions.

At the other end of Uxbridge Street, Alfred Dunhill's pipe and cigarette factory provided employment for some of the residents in the Racks. In 1918 they were advertising vacancies for learners at 14 shillings a week, experienced lady clerks at 35/- (hours 9-6), while female cigarette makers, working on piece rates, earned five shillings a thousand cigarettes.

43. Hillgate Place, known as Dartmoor Street when this photograph was taken c1900, had conditions 'worse than the East End', according to the vicar of St George's church.

The Hard-up Hollands

CONNECTING THE HIGH STREETS

Henry Richard Vassall Fox, the third Baron Holland, was in no way related to the original bearers of the Holland title, which had expired in 1721 with the death, in his early twenties, of the fourth Earl. The 200-acre Holland estate in Kensington had passed to the Edwardes family through the marriage of Elizabeth Rich (grand-daughter of the 1st Earl who had lost his head in the Civil War), but they appear not to have lived there long, and in 1726 the property was leased, as we have seen, to the notorious Henry Fox, the Whig Paymaster General. When Fox eventually succeeded in his efforts to acquire a peerage in 1768 he took his title from Holland House, his home at Kensington, of which he was soon to acquire the freehold.

The house itself was then already over 150 years old, deserted and neglected for some of that time, and badly in need of restoration. By the end of the century, when Fox's grandson took up residence, it was becoming a millstone, and in 1827 the third Baron wrote to a friend 'We are all dreadfully poor this year'.

This was only one of the many references to the financial anxieties which plagued him. Not only was the mansion on Campden Hill badly in need of repair, but it was expensive to run - at least in the manner which Lady Holland - the beautiful Elizabeth Webster - considered necessary, and the yearly bills were not covered by the modest rents received from the surrounding pastureland. In 1854 a new 21-year lease was granted for the 63 acres of Holland Farm at only £265 per annum. To bring in real money the estate had to be leased for building and this, Henry Fox decided, was certainly better than selling outright.

Before putting his plan into practice he had to settle a long-standing law suit with Lord Kensington, son of William Edwardes, the former owner, who re-

44. James Wyld's map of 1833. North of Notting Hill Gate is open countryside, with Notting Barns Farm and Portobello Farm still prominent. The Canal to Paddington has now isolated the area around Kensal Green which was, in any case administered by the parish of Chelsea.

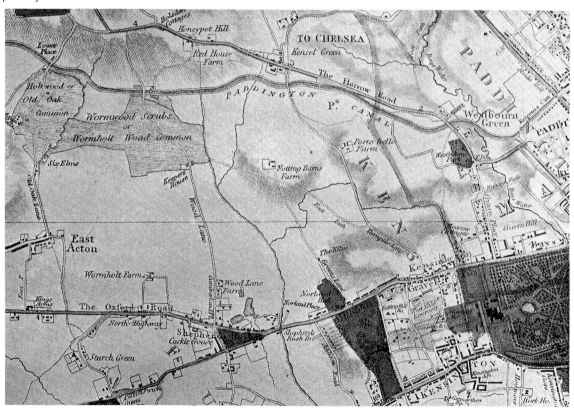

45. Elizabeth Lady Holland; portrait by Fagan.

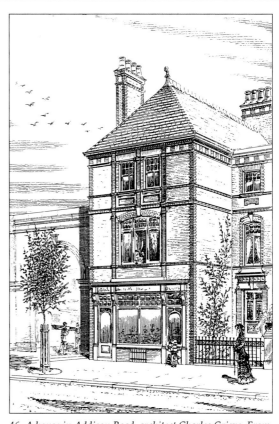

46. A house in Addison Road, architect Charles Grieve. From The Builder, *26 May 1883.*

sented his father's sale of the family estate and sought legal reasons to reclaim it. At this time the estate covered an area bounded on the east by Holland Walk, on the west by the line of the present railway, with Kensington High Street on the south and Holland Park Avenue on the north. Apart from the house and its surrounding gardens, the acreage was mostly farmland, with few buildings other than Little Holland House and Mole House, believed by the historian, Thomas Faulkner, to be the ancient West Town Manor House. Although leasing was less obnoxious than selling the land, neither Lord or Lady Holland were happy with the idea of development - he described it as a 'melancholy occupation, even if profitable', but she was pessimistic about its success anyway and, when selling of the properties proved slow, thought better returns might have been gained by leaving the land as pasture. When Addison Road was being built she wrote to her son (the future fourth Lord Holland) that although remote posterity might benefit, "none now alive will be much bettered by the undertaking".

ADDISON ROAD BUILT

Addison Road was the first throughway to link Kensington High Street with what became Holland Park Avenue, in 1823. The bend where St Barnabas church now stands circumnavigated the ponds in an area known as The Moats. These were originally fish ponds, and in all probability, those where Sir Walter Cope's cormorants performed their tricks to amuse his guests two centuries earlier; they were later converted into an ornamental lake by the owner of one of the larger houses in Addison Road, Oak Lodge. The provision of drainage proved a large initial expense: 'The sewer certainly breaks my rest, it swallows up thousands', complained Lady Holland to a friend. Building of the first houses began in 1824 and continued on and off over thirty years. The styles of dwelling varied enormously, from a modest terrace of five late-Georgian houses (nos. 27-31), now demolished and replaced by flats, to grand mansions at the northern end. No. 1 Addison Road, on the corner of Holland Park Avenue, was taken by Charles Richard Fox, (the son born to Lord and Lady Holland before their marriage, and so not eligible to succeed to the title). This house, much larger than its neighbours, had extensive grounds, part of which have now become the Holland Park Lawn Tennis Club. When Charles Fox died in 1873 the house was demolished and the land sold for speculative development, which included the Holland Park Court flats and Carlton Mansions, built in 1900.

Addison Road remained virtually unchanged from mid-Victorian times to the outbreak of the Second World War, with two exceptions: the building of Oakwood Court on the bend in 1900, and the construction of No. 8 by the progressive architect, Halsey Ricardo, for Sir Ernest Debenham in 1905. (Debenham, the West End store owner, had previously lived in another Ricardo house at the southern end of Melbury Road.) Built on the site of three earlier houses, Nos 8, 9 and 10, the new house followed the Ricardo style, being faced with glazed tiles which he considered afforded better protection against the corrosive London atmosphere than bricks. In addition to its decorative exterior the house was lavishly ornamented inside with William de Morgan tiles, marble fireplaces and intricate plasterwork. The original lease restricted occupancy to certain professions, but in 1955 permission was obtained for the house to be used as a training college for dance and drama. The Richmond Fellowship for Mental Welfare and Rehabilitation took over the house in 1965.

Lord Holland died in 1840, leaving Holland House and the estate to his widow, who continued her extravagant lifestyle to the consternation of her son, the fourth Lord Holland, who was desperate to preserve the family mansion - 'the most anxious wish of my life'. But by 1845 he was contemplating that 'dear old HH must be sacrificed or at least beset by building', and when he succeeded to the estate that year, after his mother's death, development continued, not only in Addison Road, but in side streets. By the time of his own death in 1859 much of the area was under construction or completed. One of his last transactions was with the brothers William and Francis Radford (already engaged in the development of Pembridge Gardens and Square) to build eighty large detached houses on land on the northern boundary of the estate. This great horseshoe-shaped development, with a lengthy central mews and stables was, confusingly, named 'Holland Park'. The houses were as grand as anything in London - some of them had thirty rooms. Their occupants included a peer, an Italian prince, merchants of the West Indies, East India Company and Australia, barristers, brokers and other wealthy professionals. Lord Radford stipulated that the Radfords were to construct 'good proper and substantial dwellings', costing at least £2,000 each to build, and he also made it a condition that all the large trees on the site should be preserved.

All but three of these houses survive; No. 80 was

47. Originally known as Lord Holland's Lane, Holland Walk was a sunny place for nursemaids to chat in Edwardian days.

replaced by a block of flats, Duke's Lodge, in 1939; and Nos. 1 and 1a were demolished after war damage. No. 1 had been lavishly decorated by artists such as William Morris and Walter Crane, and some of this work can still be seen at the Victoria and Albert Museum.

The extension of the West London Railway and the building of Addison Road station in 1864 saw the last parcels of land between the railway lines and Addison Road rapidly developed (within ten years over 300 houses were built, mainly by two partnerships). Amongst the last were thirty-one cottages without gardens, called Lorne Gardens, erected between 1870-74 behind the grander houses of Upper Addison Gardens, Holland Park Avenue and Holland Road. To protect the privacy of their richer neighbours the houses in Lorne Gardens were built without back windows.

The last Lady Holland not only inherited her husband's property but also his debts and mortgages and was often tempted to take desperate measures to solve her financial troubles. It was revealed later that in 1864 she contemplated selling off all the remaining grounds of Holland House for building, a plan which would have surrounded the mansion with a grid of roads; this scheme was abandoned during the property slump of 1866. By 1878 the only open land left on the Holland estate, apart from the gardens around the house, was along the route now occupied by Abbotsbury Road, the west side of which became a tennis club until 1939, when part of it was used by members of the Fire Service to keep pigs and chickens and to grow vegetables. The final development in the area did not happen until the 1970s.

HOLLAND WALK

In the early 19th century a meandering footpath connected Kensington High Street with what became Holland Park Avenue; for the most part it lay to the east of the Holland House parkland, but then diverted west across the front of the house itself to end near the vicinity of today's Ilchester Place. In 1847 Kensington Vestry persuaded the last Lord Holland to allow the footpath to be straightened so as to meet the High Street opposite Earls Court Road, and thus Holland Walk came into being.

However, Holland's widow was not so happy at the freedom of the hoi-polloi to walk so near her house and by 1854 the *Kensington Gazette* was receiving letters which described the Walk as a 'dark sink hole', dismal and dangerous owing to the erection of high fences on either side, and the lack of lighting. This 'boarded pass leading to Lord Holland's Avenue', which had been 'a delightful promenade', was now 'owing to the hideous height of these jail-like

48. Autumn time in Holland Walk. A photograph in about 1920.

walls of wood, excluding the light and air of heaven and cherishing up fogs and damps'. A correspondent wrote of the 'apprehension of insecurity being such that wives and daughters had to be warned not to use it' and he asked that the fence should be reduced to half its height. Another writer complained of the condition of the steep rough path and the absence of lighting, so that one not only stumbled over tree roots but was 'constantly afraid of the forbidding presence of a thug'. It was, he said, a 'rendezvous for the obscene'.

Lord Holland had also promised the Vestry that he would preserve the uninterrupted view over the park 'until it was laid out for building' and when trees and shrubs joined the high fences along the Walk the Vestry decided that his promise had been broken. In 1860 the Vestry ordered its own officers to remove the foliage, an action which resulted in a lawsuit for trespass which the Vestry lost.

Holland Walk was the scene of a serious robbery one afternoon in October 1772. Later the same day, between 9 and 10pm, Lady Mary Coke, of Aubrey House, recorded hearing the report of a pistol while reading in her library, which proved to be the shooting of a highwayman on the road outside her grounds.

49. *The Vestry officers cricket team which played against Kensington Vestrymen in Holland Park on 29 June 1895.*

Cows and Cricket

At the turn of this century cows were brought daily down from Ilchester Place to be milked. The animals belonged to Holland Park Farm whose last tenants were Edmund Charles Tisdall and Elizabeth Tonks, his sister-in-law. Tisdall, one of the best-known dairy farmers in suburban London, also owned a larger farm at Epsom; in 1847 he had married Amelia Tonks, daughter of another dairy farmer in South Kensington. Tisdall was also a prominent member of Kensington Vestry and renowned for his oratory; he was a founder of the Metropolitan Dairymen's Association and of the Temperance Permanent Building Society.

He was also a keen cricketer. In the summer of 1855 a cricket match was played at Holland Farm between a team chosen by H. Prinseps Esq (brother of the artist, Val Prinseps), whose family lived in Melbury Road, and one recruited by Tisdall, whose team won by 32 runs. A report in the *Kensington Gazette* refers to a 'curious incident' when the 'worthy bowler, Mr Smallbone, being come into the field quite lame from a bruise he received under his knee and being under medical advice was allowed to have a man to run for him, but no sooner had he hit the ball, such is the exhilaration of the game, that his lameness and the doctor were forgotten and he started running and

arrived at the wicket before his deputy.' Mr Smallbone continued enthusiastically and also managed to take seven wickets of the gentlemen's side in the two innings. A return match was contemplated but only 'when the gentlemen will be in better practice'.

Cricket was played at Holland Park some years earlier. It is recorded that in 1848, Mrs Johnson of Holland Farm agreed to let one of her fields to the pioneers of 'gentlemen's cricket' in Kensington, for a rent of £15 per annum. This charge was considered to be reasonable ('owing to its proximity to London') and Lord Holland gave his blessing and even became President of the new club. A gardener, a Mr Dryx, was engaged 'from among men accustomed to preparing cricket grounds' at a fee of £12 a year and a Mr Guest, a carpenter, was contracted to put up an oaken gate. Other 'cricketing necessities' were obtained from the late Clarence Cricket Club, including a tent for £7, and a flagstaff was presented by an anonymous benefactor. The club rules prohibited members from smoking during a game. Unfortunately the organisation survived only three years - its annual dinners apparently receiving better support than the matches, all of which are recorded in their Minute Book still in the possession of a descendant of one of the founders, Edward Cortazzi, of Edwardes Square, the club's most spectacular bowler.

Sensations and Crimes

DEATH OF A CHARTIST

In September 1855, Feargus O'Connor, the Chartist leader, demented and impoverished, died in a Notting Hill lodging-house, bringing to an end the story of the Chartist movement, and its threat to the privileged that had lurked for over sixty years. In his prime O'Connor had been a giant of a man with a style and voice to match. He led his supporters to the brink of rebellion; claiming descent from kings of Ireland, he had harangued crowds in Palace Yard, Westminster. He boasted that he 'would smarten up the poor working classes who were too dirty to sit in the Commons, but if he 'washed them, kitted them out in new suits and perfumed them with the latest fashionable stink', they would prove 'the best 658 men who ever sat there.'

A verdict of natural causes was recorded at his inquest and there was a public collection to pay for his funeral. The *Kensington Gazette*, reporting the inquest, distinguished him from all the other poor Irishmen who perished in the back rooms of Notting Hill's sleazier streets. The jury had been asked to view the body again as O'Connor's nephew claimed that 'it showed a great want of care', but the coroner was satisfied. Hearing that the deceased's sister could

50. Feargus O'Connor

not pay for the interment, the Superintendent of a lunatic asylum where O'Connor had been an inmate, offered to advance the necessary sum and a juryman offered to contribute a pound. The burial took place on 10 September, 1855 at Kensal Green Cemetery. The *Kensington Gazette* was there: 'The friends and admirers of the deceased in his early political movements, mustered in strong force at the Prince Albert, Notting Hill, and followed the corpse two abreast to the cemetery where an oration was delivered over the deceased's body by a working man.'

At about this time fights between Irish boys from Kensal Road and from Lisson Grove were a common occurrence. More serious were confrontations between residents of Notting Hill and Irish immigrants, when the favourite challenge was "Who are you for? The Pope or Garibaldi?" A riot of this kind happened in 1860 in Middle Row, when two hundred police assembled beside the canal and there were many arrests.

A fatal and celebrated duel was fought in Holland Park in 1804 between Lord Camelford and Captain Best. The eccentric Camelford, aroused by some comments Best had made about a lady friend of his, challenged Best to a duel, not knowing that his opponent was one of the best shots in England; the outcome was that Camelford was killed.

SOME FAMOUS MURDERS

One of the most publicised murders of the 1920s was that of Vera Page, who was found dead and brutally assaulted in the driveway of one of the large houses at the northern end of Addison Road. Near her body was found a finger-stall, smelling strongly of ammonia, and this led back to Vera's home in Blenheim Crescent where above the Pages lived a couple whose son was friendly with Vera's parents. He worked at a laundry where ammonia was often used and a few days before her death had cut his finger. He made no secret of this, but denied that the stall belonged to him. Despite extensive investigation (the police claimed that over 18,000 people had been interviewed), the murder was never solved.

Over thirty years later, Kelso Cochrane, a 32-year-old West Indian carpenter, living in Bevington Road, North Kensington, also met a violent death, and an injured finger also had a part to play in that tragedy. On 16 May, 1957, Cochrane, who had hurt his hand at work, went to the Casualty department at Paddington Hospital late at night because he was in pain. After treatment he went out into the Harrow Road and a little while later a taxi driver saw a 'scrimmage' at the corner of Golborne Road and Southam Street. As he approached, one of the men, Cochrane, collapsed and an hour and a half later died from a stab wound in the chest. This crime, too, remained unsolved, and when Cochrane was buried at Kensal

Green over a thousand mourners from the West Indian community followed his coffin.

There was no mystery about another brutal murder which took place in Notting Hill on 1 June, 1946, when a chambermaid found Margery Gardner dead in a bedroom of the Pembridge Court Hotel. The man with whom she had arrived the previous night, Neville Heath, had already left and would kill again before he was caught. His second victim was a young Wren, whom he met at Bournemouth. He was executed in October that year.

Ruston Close, until its destruction to make way for Westway, was a cul-de-sac on the western side of St Mark's Road, just before its junction with Lancaster Road. But this was not its original name for it was once Rillington Place, where John Reginald Christie and his wife took a flat at No. 10 in 1938. The story of Christie is infamous in the history of crime. He was finally accused of the murders of at least eight women in the house, and there is a strong probability that he was also responsible for the murder of a child for which another tenant, Timothy Evans, had already been hanged. The case of Evans was always a potent weapon in the campaign to abolish capital punishment.

Prominent in that campaign for the removal of the death penalty was Mrs Violet Van der Elst, who devoted thirty years to the cause. She lived in one of the larger houses in Addison Road, known as The Lodge, which became the focus of media attention each time an execution was imminent. As each death sentence was handed down she organised protests, meetings and demonstrations, sometimes employing dozens of sandwich-men to carry placards, with marching bands playing hymns; on the mornings of executions she and others would keep silent vigil outside the prison. She was not opposed to severe punishment for murderers, but she deplored the 'life-for-a-life' concept.

The extraordinary Mrs Van der Elst was also a self-made millionaire, hypnotist, composer, portrait painter, pioneer aviator and compulsive litigant. Before she moved to Addison Road in 1932 she lived at 4, Palace Gate, the former home of Baron Rothschild, where she began the first hydro in Britain, fitted out with pale green marble baths in which clients could lie in water imported from continental spas. Her Addison Road home was no less opulent. It contained over three hundred priceless Chinese lacquered and hand-painted panels decorating the walls of a 'Chinese Room'. Elsewhere there were antique mandarin chairs, exquisite ivories and four giant Chinese god figures encrusted with gems. The library contained over 3,000 books on witchcraft and magic. When her second husband died in 1934 she kept his body in a lead coffin in the basement for over a year, seeking consolation in her grief by attending seances.

51. *The funeral of Kelso Cochrane at Kensal Green Cemetery in 1957.*

52. *Rillington Place (later renamed Ruston Close and now demolished) as it was in Christie's day.*

Her campaign against capital punishment was born out of a desire to devote the rest of her life to a cause that would have gained his approval. She stood for election to Parliament three times, promising that if chosen there would be more excitement in the House of Commons than ever before and that if she were ejected for bad behaviour she would climb back through a window again. Sadly for British political history, this did not happen and she died a recluse, frail and almost penniless.

In more recent times a tragedy which shocked the world of art and literature was the brutal murder in his home at 9 Ladbroke Grove of James Pope Hennessy. The 58-year-old writer and critic died on 25 January 1974 at the hands of an assailant who was described as an 'associate' of the young men Hennessy came into contact with through his 'risky life style'.

53. Edge Street; view looking west from the top end. In the background is the waterworks tower and St George's church. Watercolour by Mrs E. Gladstone, 1890.

Around the Great Grey Tower

In 1970 the 'great grey tower' on Campden Hill, immortalised by G.K. Chesterton, came crashing down - conservationists lost this battle. Chesterton made Notting Hill his 'Holy Mountain' in his allegorical work, *The Napoleon of Notting Hill*, in which armies of various parishes or 'free cities' of west London struggle for survival, led by their hero, Adam Wayne. 'Pump Street', which Adam refuses to surrender is relevant to present-day campaigns to preserve good old buildings. The water tower, which dominated the skyline there for over a century, was demolished as modern methods of supply made it unnecessary.

The story of reservoirs on Campden Hill begins in 1809, when 3 acres of the 'Racks' on the old Campden House estate were sold to the West Middlesex Water Company. The area formed a rectangle now bounded by the backs of the houses in Peel Street, Kensington Place, Kensington Church Street and Campden Hill Road. A reservoir on the site was completed quickly.

54. The water tower, Campden Hill, 1857-8. Designed by Alexander Fraser and immortalised by G.K. Chesterton as the 'great grey tower'.

Many years later the Grand Junction Water Company, looking also for a site for a reservoir, decided that Campden Hill was suitable. By then the area was built up or under development and the only open land was that which surrounded some of the more imposing villas, such as Elm Lodge, the home of Sir James McGrigor, who had been chief of the medical staff in Wellington's army during the Peninsular War. McGrigor, anxious to move to Harley Street, was eager to sell, and it was his house, together with some freehold land to the north, that became the site for a second water works. But in 1852 the Metropolitan Water Act ruled that all reservoirs within five miles of St Paul's had to be covered; this led to construction work at the Grand Junction's works at Campden Hill and the erection of the famous tower. It was built of grey brick, with an ornamental Italianate campanile top. *The Companion to The Almanac* for 1858 complimented the Company for having added 'a conspicuous architectural feature to their new works in the shape of a not inelegant tower'.

In 1904, both water companies were absorbed by the Metropolitan Water Board, established to take over all the private companies in the London area, and thereby take the profit motive out of the supply of water. In 1923 the West Middlesex reservoir was declared redundant; its western section became a garage and since then has been developed for housing. The remainder was sold to the LCC to build Fox School and the Kensington Institute in Edge Street. The Grand Junction land was also built over, apart from the covered reservoir which was already being used by the Campden Hill Lawn Tennis Club.

55. *Tower Cressy, a folly in Aubrey Road, built for Thomas Page, the civil engineer responsible for Westminster Bridge. It was intended to be a tribute to the Black Prince, whose emblems embellished its exterior. In 1944 the house was seriously damaged by a bomb and demolished shortly afterwards.*

56. *View of the water tower from Campden Hill Road*

57. *Campden Hill Square is one of the attractions of the water tower area. From 1823 it was developed by Joshua Hanson, who himself lived at No. 2 - the square was called Hanson Square at the time. When his interest in the development was sold the name was changed to Notting Hill Square and, in response to a petition of residents, altered again in 1893 to its present name to escape the association with Notting Hill. The garden was run by a Committee set up in 1832; its records show that between 1864 and 1868 there were several schools using the large houses in the Square and the Committee introduced strict rules precluding pupils from playing in the garden. Specifically, hoops, cricket, football, quoits, trap and ball, archery, catapults, throwing stones, hide-and-seek, throwing ball and kites were banned. In 1905 the residents had to cope with a rather different problem. The steep gradient here attracted the drivers of motor cars who used it as a trial ground for the capabilities of their vehicles.*

The Road to the Church

To the east of the northern part of Church Street lay the glebe land of the vicar of Kensington - ground assigned to the incumbent as part of his benefice. Four vicarages are known to have been built on the southern portion of this land: that in the early 17th century stood at the junction with Vicarage Gate; this was followed by a new building in Georgian times, and in 1877 a new house was erected further to the east where the present Vicarage and parish hall now stand in the Vicarage Gate cul-de-sac.

When the vicar of Kensington came to an agreement with a property developer in 1854 for the exploitation of the glebe lands, he stipulated that no occupants should pursue any trade that 'would prove hazardous, noisy, noisome, or offensive, including those of bagnio [brothel implied] keeper or sheriff's officer'. Even a century later the Kensington Church Street Association kept a wary eye on those who acquired shops in the area, strictly limiting retailers outside the antique and art gallery trade to essential suppliers such as grocers and chemists.

Between the glebe hands and the southern end of Church Street stood Sheffield House, on land which

58. The Royal Court Galleries, 61a Kensington Church Street, 1920s. An early antique shop in the street.

59. The Gravel Pits Almshouses near Kensington Church Street, c1820. Drawn by Robert Banks.

had belonged to the Sheffield family from the mid 17th century. A hundred years later it was sold to a builder, John Barnard, and a bricklayer, Thomas Calcott, who demolished the old house and used its gardens as a brickfield. In 1791, Thomas Robinson, a gardener to George III, purchased the estate, built a

large three-storey brick house there and this remained in his family until 1854 when it was demolished by a great nephew to add its grounds to the glebe land he was developing to the east. This was welcomed by the editor of the *Kensington Gazette*, who greatly disliked the high walls which surrounded many of the large houses in the area, including Sheffield House. 'There might be some who will miss this inelegant structure,' he opined, 'but those who anticipate the coming years already see a range of delightful dwellings and watch the going of many over their thresholds and catch the laughter and song trilling from a thousand tongues.' These idyllic houses are represented today by those in Palace Gardens Terrace, Brunswick Gardens, Berkeley Gardens and Strathmore Gardens.

In 1954 the Church Commissioners purchased the freehold of this glebe area, the vicar of Kensington retaining only the vicarage and its large garden. When the modern vicarage was built in 1966-68 the site of the earlier house became a block of flats, Hamilton House. Winchester Court was built in 1935 on the site of the house of a 19th-century property owner, F. Magniac, which in its turn was converted first into a convent, then into the orphanage of St Vincent de Paul.

Another mansion, Craven House, stood on the east side of Church Street at its northern end, on a site between No. 128 and the corner of the Mall. Bought by William, first Earl of Craven, it passed to another member of his family after his death in 1669 and was demolished in 1736 to build twelve houses, only a few of which remain, some very much altered both inside and out. (Nos. 128 and 130 are nearest to their original appearance.)

Stephen Pitt, son of a City merchant, bought 16 acres of the old Campden House estate in 1751, having already acquired a small portion of it through marriage. The latter area included Orbell's Buildings and Bullingham House, one of which was the home of Sir Isaac Newton in the last years of his life. It was

not until the 1840s that a Pitt descendant was able to capitalise on this purchase when, in the 1840s, he leased a large area and work began on the frontage with Church Street (Nos 67-81), Hornton Street, Gordon Place, Sheffield Terrace, Gloucester Walk, Tor Gardens, Campden Road and Pitt Street. These streets were disrupted in 1864 when the Metropolitan Railway built a tunnel beneath some of them.

60. *Kensington Church Street c1904.*

61. *Vicarage Gardens c1904 with car, registration number A5314.*

Catching the Train

A RAILWAY INTRUDES

When Lord Holland heard in 1836 that plans were afoot to construct a railway along the western borders of his estate, then being developed with housing, he was horrified. 'It will destroy the comfort of all who have recently built and will discourage all further buildings', he wrote. 'There appears to be no real public object in occasioning all this mischief.'

The new Birmingham, Bristol & Thames Junction Railway succeeded the failed canal enterprise instigated in 1828 by William Edwardes, the third Lord Kensington, and Sir John Scott Lillie, which utilised two miles of Counter's Creek from its outlet into the Thames, to a basin just south of Counter's (Addison) Bridge. Partly because of the advent of railways, the canal was shortlived, but the original owners, together with a local landowner and developer, Robert Gunter, switched their investment into a railway company to connect the canal basin with both the London North Western Railway and Great Western.

The plan was to construct the line on a 23ft-high viaduct, a concept which added to Lord Holland's alarm. It would, he said, 'interrupt the view of the new houses and villas in and near Addison Road and the noise and smoke and other annoyances will drive the tenants from their habitations'. The plan was later changed to lay the rails along the creek bed, although this necessitated the rerouting of the stream as a sewer beneath Holland Road.

Despite Holland's early disapproval a deal was struck with him to allow the railway across his land, although he still referred to it in a letter to his son as 'your accursed railway', and in 1840 he had to take legal action to recover money still due from the railway company which, by then, was in financial difficulties. The railway's failure - sometimes it took only £15 per month - was a popular joke; frequent lampooning in that journal earned it the nickname 'Punch's Railway' (the official title had already been shortened to the West London Railway). Passenger traffic was suspended in 1844 and the line was leased to the London Birmingham & Great Western Railway for freight transport. In 1861, however, passenger traffic was resumed when the widow of the

62. Addison Road (now Olympia) Station early this century

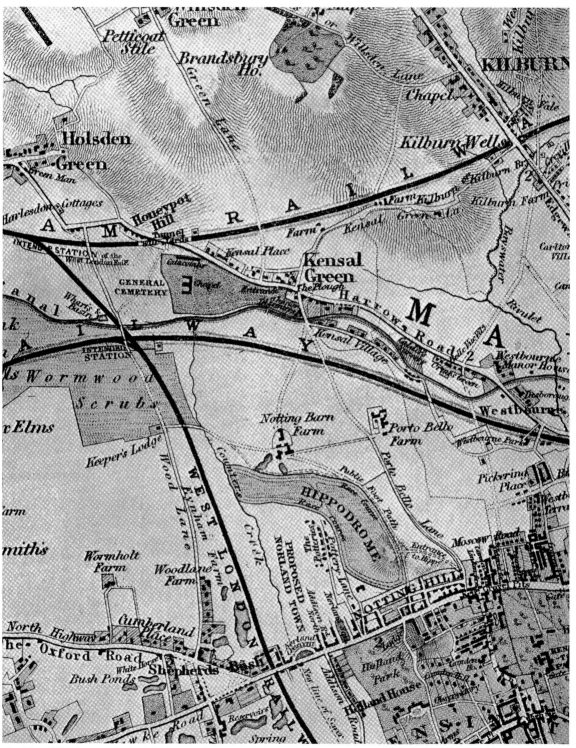

63. *Map of Kensington 1841 by E.R. Davies, showing the railway system actual and intended.*

64. *Travellers at Addison Road station. An undated photograph.*

fourth and last Lord Holland leased land to the London & North Western Railway Company to provide a station at Addison Road (now Olympia).

At about the same time as 'Punch's Railway' was being constructed, another line was built to the north of Notting Hill. In 1832 work began to join the GWR line from Bristol with the London & Birmingham Railway near Kensal Green, with a joint terminus at Euston, although this was later altered to Paddington to take advantage of the Grand Junction Canal basin there. Construction involved the excavation of a tunnel beneath the new Kensal Green Cemetery and in the *Mirror* of 28 April, 1838 a writer commented on the contrast between the two enterprises: 'the clear yet chilling note of the cemetery chapel bell has to compete with the almost indescribable noise of the approaching engine and its train upon the railway many yards beneath'.

The construction of this line isolated a strip of land between it and the canal which was eventually used to build the Western Gas Company works (later the Gas, Light & Coke Company).

Lord Holland was wrong about the railway. In fact, property values tended to go up with a railway station in the vicinity. This is evident in an 1870 advertisement for new houses in Ladbroke Grove, said to be 'most conveniently situate and especially deserving of the attention of gentlemen engaged in business in the City, the facilities afforded by the Hammersmith and City Railway in connection with the whole Metropolitan system, affording the means of speedy access to all parts of London, Ladbroke Grove station is within a few seconds' walk of the property'.

The Hammersmith & City Railway, crossed the brickfields and swamps of Notting Dale on a viaduct built by over 300 imported navvies. Opened in 1864, it provided a link between Farringdon Street in the City and Hammersmith, via Paddington and the GWR Green Bridge Station (Westbourne Park), and a branch line from Latimer Road to the West London Railway. There was a 30-minute service and the return fare was sixpence.

65. Interior of Notting Hill Metropolitan line station, c1868.

66. *Exterior of Notting Hill Metropolitan line station, c1868.*

BUSES AND COACHES

The Great Exhibition of 1851 gave a boost to horse bus travel and led to an unscrupulous raising of fares, but in 1869 the *Kensington News* reported that 'while the Bayswater omnibus conveys passengers from Notting Hill to Regent's [Oxford] Circus for threepence the omnibus company is bewailing its decline of fortune'. Competition was obviously keen with the 'Halfpenny Bus' ('and very smart and pretty they are too' said the *News*) taking passengers on four stages for a halfpenny. Climbing to the top deck of these early vehicles was a difficult and delicate business for women but in the 1860s 'decency boards' were introduced along the sides to protect them from curious males.

London's first tram - a short-lived experiment - was run by an American, aptly called George Train, from Marble Arch to Bayswater in 1861. It was not a popular innovation - apart from the noise which residents complained of, the rails protruded *above* the road surface, making travel hazardous for horses. Steam buses never fully established themselves and were, in any case, hampered initially by the Locomotives Act 1865 - the famous Red Flag Act - which restricted speeds to 2mph in towns, with the vehicle in question preceded by a man carrying a red flag. By

the time that speed restrictions were relaxed the motor bus had entered into the competitive fray, but in 1902 the London Road Car Company did begin an experimental steam bus service between Hammersmith and Oxford Circus, via Notting Hill Gate, which was immediately christened the 'twopenny lodging house' after both its fare and the time it took to complete its journey.

THE COMING OF THE UNDERGROUND

The Metropolitan Railway, which opened from Paddington to Farringdon Street in 1863, was the first underground railway in the world. Twenty years had elapsed since Charles Pearson had first presented his idea of a rail line beneath the City of London's crowded streets; he made no money out of his bold scheme and died six months before the opening date. In 1868 the line was extended from Paddington to South Kensington via Bayswater and Notting Hill, using tunnels under many of the newly-built houses. In Pembridge Square some of the properties had to be supported by iron girders beneath the basement kitchens. In the *Kensington News* in 1869 it was reported that 'owing to the supposed shaking of the railway as the principal cause, four houses in the occupation of small tradesmen in Westbourne Park

67. *Notting Hill Gate Central line station, c1900.*

Passage fell on Thursday. Happily without any injury to life or person.' Gardens were a problem as well. A lady correspondent in Kensington noted 'the decline of shrubs and foliage which awhile since adorned many spots in Kensington' and blamed this on the smoke of the passing trains.

At this time the trains of the Metropolitan line were, indeed, steam trains. Passengers also suffered from sulphurous fumes in overcrowded carriages which had little ventilation and an unstable gaslighting system. The gas frequently gave out, plunging the carriages into darkness and aiding the work of pickpockets. When passengers complained the guard told them to 'come out if you don't like it'. Other discomforts have modern connotations. The *Kensington News* in 1869 remarked that 'Every night the ears of travellers upon local lines are dinned by the discordant sound scraped upon worn violin strings, ground from concertinas, keys banged from ancient tambourine parchments with clapper accompaniment, blown through trombones or tooted upon cornets...With dull lights in the carriages, stopping of trains in the dark tunnelling and the obscene talk of soldiers, now to be seen in nearly all third class carriages, the journey by the Slow and Sewer is surely bad enough without these instruments.'

Although the developers of the Ladbroke Grove estate were confident that the proximity of the railway would help to sell their houses, even the sixpenny fare was too much to encourage the working classes to live out of London, and a popular campaign was instigated to get cheap fares for early

morning travel. The leader of the movement in west London was a Latimer Road newsagent, Charles Maggs, who informed the *Kensington News* that it was months since the new Latimer Road station had opened but builders were in a 'state bordering on bankruptcy, tradesmen were wasting their hardearned capital and on all sides new houses were going to ruin for want of occupants.' The reason he gave for the reluctance of working men to leave their 'vermin-infested houses with little or no comfort or convenience' was only the want of cheap fares. (These were, of course, introduced, and continued until after the Second World War.)

68. *Notting Hill Gate Metropolitan line station, shortly before its demolition*

Unwillingly to School

EDUCATING THE POOR

The opportunity of education for most poor children before the 19th century came from the Church. The duty of the vicar (or more likely his curate) was to instruct the children of the parish in the scriptures, which would entail reading and writing; some of the more zealous would throw in a little arithmetic as well. Kensington was more fortunate than many areas in its facilities for the education of its children. In the early 17th century there were two 'instructors of youth in the parish', and 'two poor men which teacheth children, sometimes they have few scholars, sometimes none, but men of honest behaviour and sound religion.'

In 1705 two beneficent ladies, Catherine Dicken and Mary Carnaby, left £90 to the parish school in their wills and in 1707 this and other bequests were joined together and a subscription raised to fund a charity school. Queen Anne, a local resident, subscribed £50 and her husband, Prince George of Denmark, £30 for the schoolmaster's salary.

The school was run by a Board of Trustees and subscribers were allowed to nominate pupils. The boys wore a uniform of 'shutes with briches of blew leather, coats of warm kersie, linen shirts and bands, woollen hose and buckled shoes'. The girls wore 'gounds of Padua serge, blue aprons and quoiffs, riding hoods and pattens'. The boys also had 'woollen caps with crimson tosses at the top and crimson strings'. When the old schoolroom near the parish church became too small a new one was built in 1711 on the same site, designed by Nicholas Hawksmoor. Its situation in Kensington High Street ensured that most of its pupils would come from the village itself, including the children of the servants at the several large houses, but it is likely, too, that the sparse population from the gravel pits area of Notting Hill would have used it as well.

In the early 1800s two organisations were founded to provide elementary education for poor children. Both had a religious basis and much of the tuition revolved around the Bible. The National Schools, run by the National Society for the Education of the Poor in the Principles of the Established Church, were rivalled by the non-conformist British Schools, but both agreed to share a government grant of £24,000 made by Parliament in 1824. Many of these schools charged fees of a few pennies but even this amount excluded the abject poor who, in many cases, were unwelcome owing to their insanitary condition. It

69. *Charity School, Kensington High Street, c1711; designed by Nicholas Hawksmoor. On the site of the old Town Hall.*

was to serve their needs that Ragged Schools were set up and they proved to be their only hope of education, especially in the northern parts of Notting Hill where the settlement of working people in the mid 19th century became significant.

One of the earliest of these schools was the Norland and Potteries Ragged School, opened in 1858 by Lord Shaftesbury, who in 1844 had helped to organise a Union of Ragged Schools. Another was opened in 1862 in Colville Mews, to be succeeded by All Saints Parochial Schools. (As churches were built in these northern areas many took on the additional mission of education.) In 1839 the Kensington Infant National School was begun by the Vestry and Charity School trustees in Edge Street to serve the rapidly growing community at Notting Hill Gate. This was taken over by the newly-established district of St George's church in 1865, and continued until 1963, when it was amalgamated with Fox Schools nearby. A year after the Edge Street School had begun, Lady

Mary Fox, daughter of the third Lord Holland, and another benefactor, pioneered the opening of a National School, St James's, in the most putrid area of the Potteries, known as 'The Ocean'.

A Ragged School in Blechynden Street, known as Brown's School, had doubled in size by 1866 when the new church of St Clement's opened its National School nearby. Brown's School was named for the London City Missioner, S.R. Brown, who had been appointed in 1861 'to visit in the new poor houses north of the Potteries' where a schoolroom had been closed down for the building of the railway line. The one small classroom was situated in the Mission Hall, which stood in the midst of a 'primeval swamp which could only be crossed by a narrow path marked by white posts'. Another non-conformist Mission school was set up in Bosworth Road in a tiny place only 21 feet long, 12 feet wide and 9 feet high, with one small window.

The 1870 Education Act made elementary schooling for all children a statutory obligation through the National School Board. To the children of families living eight or more to a room in the festering slums of the Dale, the large new brick buildings with their cupolas and minarets, which still survive all over London, must have seemed like palaces, however institutional.

The first Board School to be built in Notting Hill was in Wornington Road in 1874, although one for

70. A Scripture Knowledge certificate presented at the LCC Fox School in Kensington Church Street, 1914.

boys had been opened in temporary quarters in a hall in Crescent Street in 1873 near St Clement's church, moving later to a new building on the Latimer estate. The Crescent Street hall was utilised again during the building of Sirdar Road school. The original 1873 school had been considered rather high class owing to its tuppence a week fee, but when it became a Board School it was known as the Penny Board because its rough pupils were said to be bribed with sweets to attend.

71. The Standard VII class at Oxford Gardens School in 1891.

Other Board Schools were established during the next few years, some taking their pupils from Ragged Schools, others breaking new ground. Among these were Barlby Road, opened in 1880 to teach children transferred from temporary schools in Kensal Town. The site chosen was hardly salubrious, having a pig slaughterhouse on one side and a carpet beater's on the other. At Oxford Gardens (1884) the leading tradesmen in the area petitioned the School Board to provide education for their children 'at the highest possible fee [sixpence a week] to keep the intake select'; fees were abolished in 1891.

Over six hundred Catholic children of families attracted to Kensal Town by the building of railways were catered for by the Roman Catholic Mission School at St Mary's in East Row in 1872, supplemented in 1878 by the Middle Row Board School which, at its height, had no less than 1,600 pupils.

It was a dilemma for Victorian intelligentsia to decide if ignorance encouraged poor people to keep to their station in life or, more inconveniently, incited them to rebellion, as had happened in France. But the more enlightened realised that Britain's future status and prosperity rested not only on its political and military might but on a competent technical and artisan class, the leaders of which were unlikely to come from the middle classes. But at that stage the road to higher education for those not at universities was a difficult one, even for those with money.

PRIVATE SCHOOLS

Elsewhere in the educational system, the standard of tuition in public schools was generally of a poor standard: classics were taught by rote, the pupils endured degraded living conditions and discipline, and there was a general disinclination on the part of staff and pupils alike to take education seriously. As a consequence there was a mushrooming of private and military academies, some of which were established in Kensington and Holland Park.

One of the earliest and most ambitious was opened in 1761 by Thomas Marquois, a 'Professor of Artillery and Fortification', at Norland House on a site of 12 acres (see next page) between Portland Road, Norland Square and Penzance Place (now 131 Holland Park Avenue). This was intended for 'the civil or military education of sons of the gentry'. The curriculum included Greek, Latin, French, Writing and Arithmetic, the fees, including board and lodging, being £30 p.a. Fortification, Mathematics, Navigation, Drawing, Geography, Fencing and Riding were all extras. The establishment, which lasted until 1792, included stables, a fives court and riding areas. Alderney cows were kept to provide milk.

The Civil Service rather than the Army was the target of Wren College, established in the 1870s in Powis Square where no less than six houses were used. Wren Gurney, as it was known, coached young men to enter the Indian Civil Service, many of whom

72. Bayswater Proprietary School, Norland Square; photograph 1868.

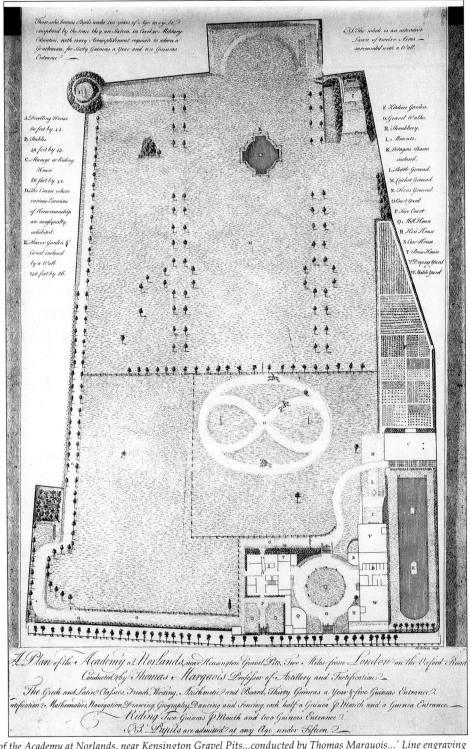

73. 'A Plan of the Academy at Norlands, near Kensington Gravel Pits...conducted by Thomas Marquois...' Line engraving by H. Roberts.

Laſt Saturday evening a fire broke out near the Military Academy at Norland-houſe, on the Acton-road, which threatened deſtruction to the whole neighbourhood, as no water could be got, or engines procured, for ſome time. It burnt with great rapidity till three houſes were conſumed. The unfortunate ſufferers are greatly indebted to the young gentlemen at the above Academy, who regularly mounted guard over that part of the property which could be faved. One of them, a Mr. Pigot, nephew to General Sir Robert Pigot, in viſiting the different poſts they had guarded, obſerving a fellow to dig up the earth behind one of the houſes on fire, aſked what he was doing; the villain anſwered, "watching the water." But ſuſpicions ariſing, the young gentlemen went to the place when he left it, and found a large quantity of plate hid, which proved a fortunate circumſtance to the diſtreſſed owners.

TO be Sold by Auction, by Mr. LANG-FORD and SON, on the Premiſes, on Tueſday the 21ſt Inſtant,

The Leaſe of the large and capital Meſſuage, uſually called NORLANDS, and lately the MILITARY ACADEMY, ſituate on the North Side of the High Road, near the Gravel-Pits, at Kenſington, in the County of Middleſex; together with the Coach-Houſes, Stables, brewhouſe, Mill-Houſe, a large Riding-Houſe newly erected; and ſeveral Out-Offices, and a fine Lawn of about ten Acres; a Kitchen Garden, and a Flower Garden of about two Acres, and two Canals well ſtocked; at the End of the Lawn are two large Mounts planted with flowering Shrubs, and the greateſt Part of it is walled in. The Premiſes are held by Leaſe for a Term, of which there are ſeventeen Years to come from Midſummer next, ſubject to the Payment of a Rent Charge of 100l. per Annum, out of which Land-Tax is to be deducted.

At the ſame Time will be ſold the managed Horſes belonging to the Riding-Houſe, all the Horſe Furniture, and four Alderney Cows.

The Horſes may be ſeen in the Manege every Day, (Sunday excepted) from Twelve o'Clock till One.

74 & 75. Newspaper cuttings relating to Norland Military Academy. The first concerns a fire in 1787, the second (no date) details the selling of the property, probably in 1792.

were of oriental or Eurasian birth and boarded in nearby streets so that the area became known as 'Little India'. Its proprietor, Walter Gurney, although a cripple, became a London County Councillor and later an MP.

St Charles' College, named for St Charles of Borromeo, was founded by Cardinal Manning in 1863 to provide private education at moderate cost for Roman Catholic youths. It began at Sutherland Place, Paddington, then moved successively to Bayswater, and then to St Charles' Square in 1874 to a purpose-built range of buildings. In red brick and stone, these were grouped around a tower 140 feet high which became a local landmark. By 1890 over a thousand students had passed though the College into various professions. In 1903 it became a college for training women teachers run by the Sacred Heart Community of nuns, and after the Second World War it was used for the Cardinal Manning Boys' School and the Sion Manning School for Girls.

There were numerous other tutorial establishments. In 1854, Mr J. Walker, 'late of Corp. Coll. Camb.' advertised in the *Kensington Gazette* that he was willing to receive a few pupils at 1 Union Terrace, Notting Hill who would be 'thoroughly prepared for public school. Day boys £1.1. a quarter, boarders £21 p.a. Books and washing being the only extras'.

As boys were sent away to boarding school the employment of a governess for their sisters became more of an extravagance and from the early years of the 19th century more and more boarding schools for girls were established, often utilising the new large houses being erected just outside London. The building which was eventually to be the Cardinal Vaughan School in Addison Road began as the Kensington Academy for Girls and Addison Hall, the latter a place for public entertainment intended to help finance the school. However, its proprietor, Mrs Mary Grant, was unable to obtain a licence for the Hall and was foreclosed by one of her mortgagees. She moved to small premises at 96 Addison Road, but the new owners were more successful and the Hall was used for various entertainments until 1914, when it was taken over by the Catholic school.

Among the earliest girls' schools was that opened at Campden House in 1751 by a Mrs Terry. Considered a very high class establishment, it drew its pupils from rich and aristocratic families. Conditions there, however, were uncongenial. When a young girl died of consumption in 1797 her father blamed her death on the school, writing that 'The rules for health are detestable, no air but in a measured formal walk, and all running and quick motion prohibited. Preposterous! The school deceptive of all sorts, the food etc. all contributed, she never had a full belly at breakfast. Detestable! This at the expense of £80 per year!'

Small schools existed in houses in such streets as Colville Square, Royal Crescent, Norland Square, Lansdowne Road, Kensington Park Gardens, Campden Hill Square, Tavistock Road and Addison Road. In May 1876 Miss Emily Lord, a young teacher at the nearby Notting Hill High School, opened a kindergarten for five children at 9 Norland Place, a terrace of houses in Holland Park Avenue (now No. 166). By 1891, when she married and handed over to

76. *The headmaster of Kensington Grammar School, the Rev. Mr Joscelyn, sits with the School Secretary among junior boys in the 1880s. The fashions of the day ranged from sailor suits to corduroys and watchchains.*

senior teachers, it accommodated nearly 100 children in two houses with a hall and extra classrooms built on. Early pupils were drawn from the area's new artistic community, such as little Margaret Burne Jones 'with lapis lazuli eyes', and Walter Crane's little daughter, Beatrice. Later pupils included George Llewellyn Davies and his brothers, for whom J.M. Barrie wrote *Peter Pan*, and Arthur Bliss, who was later to become Master of the Queen's Music. This school still survives, although it takes only junior pupils nowadays.

When Holland Park and Campden Hill were threatened by development in the 1950s the LCC compromised by designating the land for educational purposes, and Holland Park Comprehensive School, the first of its kind, came into being. Public opposition was appeased by restricting building heights, the old right-of-way footpath to Holland Walk was retained as was one of the old houses, and even old trees were carefully preserved.

EVENING EDUCATION

The first Mechanics' Institution for evening education had been founded in 1824, but it was not for thirty years that a Parochial Institute was established in Kensington the aims of which were 'to afford the opportunity for intellectual improvement by means of public lectures, a reading room, library and evening classes'. But it did not meet with much success. Possibly this was due to the subjects of the lectures - a trek to the Association's rooms at the King's Arms to hear a discourse on the *Use of Teeth in Man and Animals*, for a shilling entrance fee, was not taken lightly, especially when the same money could buy a large quantity of gin.

Classes were held every evening from 7 to 9 in the Infants' School at Edge Street to instruct young men and women in reading, writing and arithmetic, for a subscription of a guinea a year. Scientific subjects and even mathematics were seldom offered to women but in 1878 a course of lectures in Household and Domestic Science, held under the auspices of King's College in the Strand, was given at Kensington Vestry Hall. They were so well attended that they moved to a larger venue in Hornton Street, and in 1885 a King's College Women's Department was established in two houses in Kensington Square and although originally intended for instruction in Household and Social Sciences the curriculum was gradually widened. In 1914 the University of London took a 999-year lease of the site of Bute House on Campden Hill to erect the present greatly extended Queen Elizabeth College complex.

Sermons in Stones

In a period of little more than forty years, from 1845 to 1888, over a dozen Church of England churches thrust their towers and spires above the roof tops of Notting Hill; in addition, numerous non-conformist chapels and missions, and buildings for the largely Catholic immigrants, appeared.

The Church of England had become aware that all over the country there were large communities in towns and cities which had no access to a place of worship, and nowhere more so than in London, so that when Charles Blomfield became Bishop of London one of his main tasks was the setting up of a Building Fund to remedy the situation.

Other interested parties included the developers of new estates who were well aware that an imposing church in a development helped to sell the houses around it. One such in Notting Hill was Charles Henry Blake, a wealthy retired Calcutta merchant, whose later enterprises included not only housebuilding but investment in railways. Blake was

directly involved in the building of no less than four churches in fifteen years. The first of these, in 1845, was St John the Evangelist on the crest of Ladbroke hill, a site which had once been the natural grandstand for the Hippodrome racecourse; this church was known as 'St John in the Hayfields' because of its rural situation. It was the first church in Kensington built north of Holland Park Avenue; its building costs were met by private subscription, in particular by two large loans of £2,000 each from Viscount Canning and Charles Blake. The next object for Blake's entrepreneurial piety was St Peter's, Kensington Park Road, dedicated in 1855, where he presented the site; the architect, Thomas Allom, designed this church in classical Italianate style, and he also created the large classical-style houses in Blake's surrounding streets.

St Mark's, in St Mark's Road, owed its existence to its first patron, Miss E.F. Kaye, who donated £5,000 towards its building and ensured that its first incumbent was her nephew, but once again the site was donated by Blake, by now busy on the St Quintin estate. St Mark's, consecrated in 1863, followed the Anglo-Catholic liturgy of the Oxford Movement.

77. St Mark's Church, designed by Bassett Keeling. Opened in 1863, the church was declared redundant and demolished in the 1970s

78. All Saints Church, as designed by William White

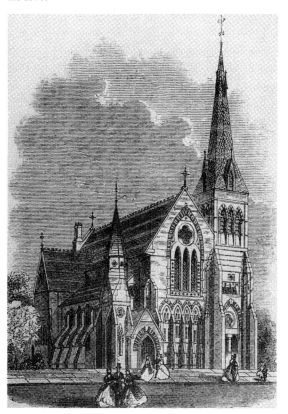

79. *St John's, Ladbroke Grove.*

The church was made redundant and demolished in the 1970s and its site is now covered by a group of houses.

Blake, working on his Portobello Estate, and his partner, John Parson, chairman of the Hammersmith & City Railway, presented the site of St Michael and All Angels church in Ladbroke Grove on condition that the building was completed in two years (presumably to match the timing of their development). The building costs were met by the father of the first incumbent, the Rev. Edward Ker Gray. From its consecration in 1871 St Michael's became a fashionable church, famous for its music, and it was frequented by members of the Royal Family; its services were advertised on the front page of *The Times* and the Duke of Edinburgh (third son of Queen Victoria) played a violin in the church orchestra. At the time of Gray's departure to take charge of the even more fashionable Curzon Street Chapel in Mayfair, the social character of the neighbourhood was going rapidly downhill, and the newsworthy heyday of St Michael's was over.

THE TROUBLES OF THE REVEREND WALKER

The Rev. Samuel Walker had been involved with Blake in some local development, but he could not be accused of materialism or humbug. A deeply religious man, he appeared solely concerned with the families whom he hoped would soon populate the area around Talbot Road. His own church, All Saints, was a focal point of Colville and Powis Squares and his vision was for a 'free and open church' which would be a spiritual centre for the area. The building, designed by William White, working with Sir George Gilbert Scott, was greatly admired, but due to Dr Walker's financial difficulties it was still far from complete when it was first used. It lacked a spire and its interior was unfurnished and undecorated, and there was, too, a matter of a £2,000 debt to the builders. (Poor Walker had envisaged a spire 'as lofty as Salisbury'.) The church's derelict state for many years earned it the nickname of 'All Sinners in the Mud'. In 1859 an attempt was made to finish it by a new incumbent, but it was still without a spire in 1861. All Saints was badly damaged by bombing in 1940, the Lady chapel and south transept chapel being destroyed, and until its restoration in 1951 the congregation was accommodated at St Columb's in Lancaster Road, a church, incidentally, named after Walker's home town, St Columb Major, in Cornwall.

The owner of the Norlands estate, Charles Richardson, promised £500 towards the cost of building St James's church there in 1844 and local residents supplied much of the balance. The church was consecrated in 1845, though the spire was still not in place. The architect was James Vulliamy, son of the clockmaker, Benjamin Lewis Vulliamy, the previous owner of the Norlands estate before it was sold to Richardson.

Colonel Matthew Chitty Downes St Quintin, a former colonel in the Lancers and owner of the Notting Barns farmlands, presented the land on which St Helen's church was built in 1874, a triangular site just off St Mark's Road, and he also contributed £1,000 towards the building costs. This church was also badly bombed in the last war but rebuilt in 1951 and united with Holy Trinity, Latimer Road, in Hammersmith.

St Helen's was the second venture of a remarkable Victorian clergyman, the Rev. Arthur Dalgarno Robinson, who had come to Notting Hill from Shepherds Bush, where he was a curate at St Stephen's. In 1862 he was instrumental in the erection of a temporary iron church, dedicated to St Andrew, at the corner of Walmer and Lancaster Roads, and the establishment of a Ragged School for children from the nearby Potteries. He used his own resources to build the modest 'village' church of St Clement's, to provide free sittings for 900 people; this was consecrated in 1867. During the whole of his first seven years in the parish he worked without pay and was held in great affection by the poverty-stricken families in the squalid alleys and streets of the area.

In 1868 Robinson persuaded the Bishop of London to grant five acres of glebe land so as to endow St Clement's, and on part of this he built a massive Parsonage House in North Pole Road, with sixteen rooms and various offices; this building survived until the 1960s. Robinson died in his parsonage in 1899, having been vicar of St Clement's for forty years, and he is commemorated in Dalgarno Gardens and Way.

Another clergyman, the Rev. E.J. May, applied to the Ecclesiastical Commissioners in 1860 to build a church at the northern end of Holland Road to meet the needs of the new residents of the Holland House estate. His appeal was rejected, possibly because St Barnabas, at the southern end of Addison Road (built in 1829), would have suffered in competition for paying pew holders. However, nine years later, another applicant, the Rev. G. Booker, succeeded where May had failed and was granted permission to erect a temporary church on a piece of land in Addison Gardens; this eventually developed into the church of St John the Baptist, opened in 1889. This church enjoyed some notoriety in 1883, when its incumbent was a man who had served two years in prison for adopting practices contrary to the Public Worship Regulation Act.

The building of St George's church on Campden Hill in 1864 was a private venture by John Bennett of Westbourne Park Villas, principally to provide a living for his son, George. The parish was created from parts of those of St Mary Abbots and St John's in Ladbroke Grove, and was intended to serve the growing population around Notting Hill Gate and the Gravel Pits. The site occupies part of the garden of Wycombe House.

Although the land for the church of St Andrew and St Philip in Golborne Road was supplied by the Bishop of London's Building Fund, the £12,000 needed to build it was donated by an anonymous 'Christian lady' of Bayswater. The design, by the renowned church architect, E. Bassett Keeling, was much praised, but this did not save it from demolition in 1967 when the parish was united with that of St Thomas, Kensal Road. St Thomas had been built in 1889, using funds accrued by the amalgamation of two City of London churches, St Thomas in the Liberty of the Rolls and St Dunstan in the West.

St Columb's in Lancaster Road, already mentioned above, was built as a temporary mission before its permanent building in 1901. It was famous for its High Church liturgy but in 1951, after its amalgamation with All Saints, the building was sold to the Serbian Orthodox Church and is now St Sava's.

THE CATHOLIC CANDLEMAKER

In 1813 the first Roman Catholic chapel to be built in Kensington since the Reformation was opened in Holland Street. Dedicated to St Mary, it was sited on land leased for 99 years from Robert Phillimore. The lessees were Richard Gillow, the first resident of Bute House, on Campden Hill, a member of a well-known Catholic family, and James Kendall, a tallow chandler, whose factory for candlemaking stood on the site of what was to become the Derry & Toms building in Kensington High Street. His company was later absorbed by the largest candlemakers in London, Price & Co, in Wandsworth.

When Father Herman (Cohen), a Jewish convert to Catholicism and teacher of the Order of Discalced Carmelites, came to London in 1862 he rented a house in Church Street on the site of today's Newton Court, and in 1865 he bought land opposite for £3,500 on which to build a church dedicated to Our Lady of Mount Carmel and St Simon Stock. Ten years later the community extended its land interests to the west of the church and it was here that the Carmelite Monastery was built in 1886, a series of five-storey buildings in the style of 16th-century northern France, connected to the church by a corridor (the Order is an enclosed one). The Carmelite church was destroyed during the last war but rebuilt to a design by Sir Giles Gilbert Scott in 1959.

North Kensington, with a large Irish population, was a target for Roman Catholic expansion. In 1857, the first of a small community of priests, the Oblates of St Charles Borromeo, opened a mission church (later St Mary and the Angels) in Moorhouse Road, Bayswater, and two years later, Dr Henry (later Cardinal) Manning, their Superior, instigated the founding of a Franciscan Convent in Portobello Road, consisting of buildings around a cloistered garden.

The Monastery of the Poor Clares in Westbourne Park Road was established in 1857, also at the behest of Cardinal Manning, and modelled on the Order of Poor Clares in Bruges. It included two chapels built back to back to accommodate both nuns and visitors. *The Builder* commented that 'it stood in a dreary wasteland of stunted trees in a desolate district'. The Convent moved to Barnet in 1970 and the site is now occupied by municipal housing.

In 1859 one of the Oblates of St Charles, the Rev. Henry Augustus Rawes, commissioned the building of St Francis church in Pottery Lane in the heart of the terrible 'Piggeries and Potteries' of the Dale. This building (to the design of John Francis Bentley, who was later to create Westminster Cathedral), must have contrasted enormously with its squalid surroundings. The Oblates also established a mission in Kensal New Town where two cottages were used as a school; this was succeeded by Our Lady of Holy Souls, also designed by Bentley, in 1880.

But undoubtedly the most ambitious Catholic venture in 19th-century Notting Hill was the establishment of the College of St Charles, intended as an answer to the Church of England's predominance in the public schools.

In the 1970s St Mary and the Angels under the leadership of its parish priest, Michael Hollings, played a prominent part in the organisation of an ambitious series of ecumenical 'Stations of the Cross' pageants through the streets of North Kensington, in which local people from all denominations enacted the principal roles; on one occasion a black youth played the part of Jesus and was 'crucified' at Wormwood Scrubs.

THE CHAPEL BUILDERS

The evangelical nature of non-conformism appealed to middle-class tradesmen, many of them from the provinces and Wales and Scotland, who had settled in Kensington and Notting Hill. The independence which had inspired them to seek a living in London was revealed also in their religious activities. In side streets their chapels multiplied, spreading a mixture of religious enthusiasm, fire and brimstone and temperance.

The earliest such chapel appears to have been in Hornton Street in 1793. On land leased to William Forsyth, gardener of Kensington Palace (of Forsythia

fame), and his friends, James Gray, the Brompton nurseryman and the piano manufacturer, John Broadwood, an Independent Presbyterian chapel flourished for over fifty years. The congregation moved to Notting Hill Gate in 1846, where they built the impressive twin-towered edifice on the corner of Kensington Park Road, named Horbury Chapel in honour of a deacon who had been born in that Yorkshire village. Their adjacent school became eventually the home of the Mercury Theatre. In 1935 the church, renamed the Kensington Temple, was taken over by the Four Square Gospel Mission and is now an Elim Pentecostal church.

In 1862 what was known as a Proprietary chapel was opened in Kensington Park Road for an Anglican clergyman called Henry Marchment. The building was burned down in 1867 and Marchment went bankrupt in his attempts to rebuild it. The carcase was later taken over by a group of Presbyterians from Mall Hall at Notting Hill Gate, and renamed Trinity Church. It is now a Peniel Chapel.

Evangelists targeted the working class area around the waterworks at Campden Hill. Three small chapels were flourishing in the 1860s; in Hillgate Street there was a Particular Baptist chapel; in Kensington Place, Bethesda Chapel, 'a labourers' church', founded by a coachmaker; and at the top end of Church Street a 'Free Christian Church' advertised its opening in the *Kensington Gazette* in 1854. This organisation

80. *Essex Church, in the Mall at Notting Hill Gate, at the time of its opening in 1887. Turbanned sikhs are among the congregation.*

proposed to 'form a Christian Church on perfectly unsectarian principles, no religious appellation (except Christianity) will be recognised, conformity to creeds and rules of faith will be dispensed with and the only qualification required for membership will be a profession of love to Christ and an obedience to his precepts.'

Some ten years later 'a large gloomy structure' of a chapel was built in Palace Gardens Terrace by Robert Offord, whose brother, John, became its first minister. This was later taken over by the Swedenborgians as their New Jerusalem Church, became a Christian Scientist church before the First World War and was finally rebuilt in its present form in the 1920s. Next door to them the Unitarians established their Essex Church (named after their original meeting place in Essex Street, off the Strand); this was rebuilt in the 1970s.

The Evangelical churches in particular were to be found in the slums of North Kensington and Notting Dale. In 1859 a Shepherds Bush Baptist congregation opened the Norland Chapel on the corner of Queensdale and Norland Roads; this later became the Christian Mission of the Rev. William Booth, and a forerunner of the Salvation Army, when it was known as Norland Castle, under the ministry of the 'Angel Adjutant', Kate Lee. The death of a woman drowned in a slurry pit in Latimer Road in 1860 was used to launch an appeal for a new mission hall in the area to bring home to the public the ghastly conditions which existed there - the Latimer Road Mission was the result.

Although such mission halls were primarily for devotional purposes, they provided physical and social care, ragged schools, day nurseries, clinics and soup kitchens. One such, the Talbot Tabernacle, is now a social centre providing service to the community in a secular guise.

A pastor called 'Bee' Wright built a tiny chapel in which to preach against Sunday trading. And a brother of the famous evangelist, Charles Spurgeon, was the first minister of a Baptist chapel opened in Cornwall Road in 1862 by Sir Samuel Morton Peto, whose firm had been working on the removal of the Crystal Palace at South Kensington. Sir Samuel was presented with one of the transepts of the exhibition hall, 'a long wooden and plaster object', which was erected at his expense on the chapel facade.

Westbourne Grove Baptist church originated with a tiny congregation that met in Church Street in the 1820s, and the Methodists in the area began when a Bayswater butcher called Hicks founded a Sunday School in Queensway, which was the site of their first chapel in 1827, before they moved to Denbigh Road.

Butchers, coalmen, builders, tradesmen, shopkeepers (Charles Derry of Derry & Toms was the founder of a North Kensington Mission), very ordinary men and women of quite extraordinary faith and energy, and sometimes of unreasonable prejudices and dogmatic bigotry, they laid the foundations of much service and goodwill which have survived into modern times, even if their little places of worship, the tin halls, the tiny brick or iron huts, have mostly been swept away or converted to secular use.

81. The Talbot Tabernacle, which carries on the tradition of service (though in secular form) which its founder, a barrister, Gordon Furlong, envisaged in 1869. Drawing by the Author.

82. *The Hippodrome, Notting Hill, c1839.*

Square Deals

A RACECOURSE IN NOTTING HILL

The Ladbrokes were one of the wealthiest families of 18th-century London. Sir Robert Ladbroke was a banker who became Lord Mayor and one of the MPs for the City, and his brother, Richard, already owned four houses and estates in Middlesex, Surrey and Essex when he also acquired four large parcels of land north of the 'road to Uxbridge' at Notting Hill in the 1750s; this farmland today is occupied by the Linden Gardens area, Pembridge Villas and Road, and the streets stretching westwards to Portland Road and north to Lancaster Road. It was during the lifetime of his heir, Richard Weller (who took the name of Ladbroke as a condition of inheritance), that much of this land was transformed into building plots.

Within three years of inheriting the estate Richard Weller Ladbroke was already planning to build, inspired by the ideas of his architect and surveyor, Thomas Allason. He envisaged a spectacular estate, focused on a central circus and other streets leading off a broad avenue (Ladbroke Grove), consisting of large detached and semi-detached houses occupied by wealthy residents, built around central 'paddocks' or garden squares. Allason was inspired by Nash's work at Regent's Park and had his plans come to fruition this Notting Hill development might have been a London showpiece. As it happened, the financial crisis of 1825 severely affected his plans, although some building took place along the main road (mostly undertaken by the builder, Joshua Flesher Hanson of Campden Hill Square). It must have been a relief to Ladbroke when, in 1840, a Mr John Whyte took a lease of 140 acres to construct a racecourse to be known as the Hippodrome, which utilised the slopes of Ladbroke hill as a natural amphitheatre.

The Hippodrome was advertised in the *Sporting Magazine* as 'an emporium even more extensive and attractive than Ascot or Epsom'. There were three courses, one for racing, one for gentlemen who wished to exercise their horses, and one for ladies, children and invalids who could hire traps and ponies. For racing events a first-class band would be in attendance and patrons were assured that 'the footpath had been secured to prevent the entry of improper persons'.

83 & 84. Two views of the Hippodrome racecourse 1838-40

Unfortunately, the immediate neighbourhood, known as the 'piggeries and potteries', was also the home of a large encampment of gipsies, and this soon had a bad effect on the status of the venture. The path to the course became known as 'Cut-throat Lane', owing to footpads waiting to pounce on wealthy visitors, and a growth of sleazy betting booths and gin shops added to the deterioration.

Two stewards of the course, Lord Chesterfield and Count D'Orsay tried to change the image of the place by altering its name to Victoria Park, Bayswater, but this was no sop to Kensington Vestry, which threatened to close a public right of way and petitioned Parliament to close the course. In the end Whyte had to move the entrance to the course to comply with the right of way, promise to reform 'certain evils', admit the public free on Sundays and charge only twopence admission on special holidays. By 1842 he was in such a poor financial state from his various misfortunes (to make matters worse it had been discovered that the soil of the course was heavy clay, which made riding impossible at certain times), that he had to close it and hand the land back to the Ladbrokes.

85 & 86. Two views published in The Illustrated London News *of the gipsies encamped near Latimer Road 1879-80.*

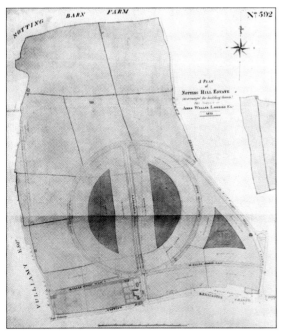

87. Plan for building on the Ladbroke Estate, by T. Allason, 1823.

A LEAFY LADBROKE

Despite financial crises, bankruptcies and debts, the great 'leafy Ladbroke' estate envisaged by Allason proceeded slowly, although the circus feature was never really completed owing to piecemeal building by speculators, but much of the vision of elegant houses in garden settings survived. Many of the more spectacular houses were the work of Thomas Allom, whose talent may be seen especially in Kensington Park Gardens and Stanley Crescent. The developer was rewarded by attracting residents of the upper middle class - merchants, surgeons, army officers and civil engineers. They were given the right of access to the communal gardens for rents from one to three guineas a year, but their servants were forbidden entry 'unless in attendance on the children or other members of the family'.

Large sums had to be expended on the sewerage and drainage of this steeply-sloping area. In 1846 a great mass of clay, 20 foot deep, which had been piled up during road construction, slid down, destroying vaults and sewers.

The earlier inspiration of Regent's Park was complemented by that of Cheltenham through one of that

88. A proposed Swiss villa in Kensington Park Road, by E.T. Dolby.

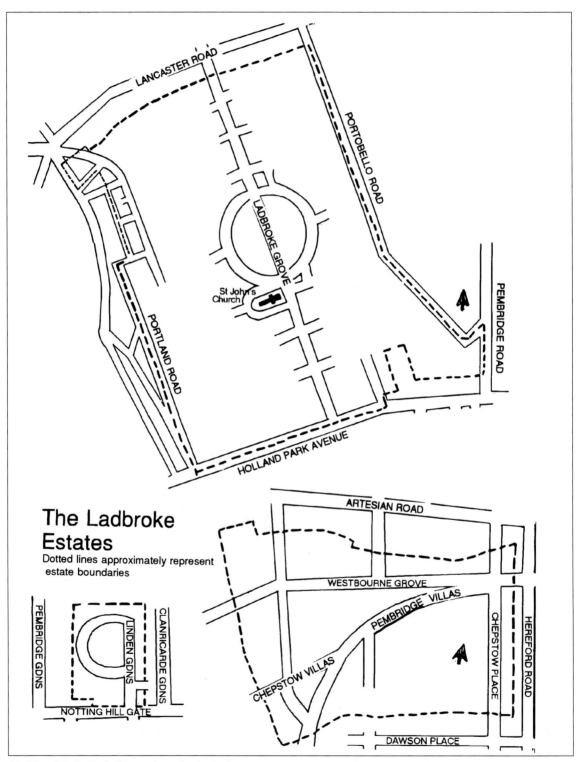

89. Map of the Ladbroke Estates, drawn by the Author.

town's most reputable citizens, the solicitor Pearson Thompson, who was an associate of one of the estate's most prominent speculators, Richard Roy. Not that the venture was particularly successful for Thompson, for when he was about to emigrate to Australia in 1849 he declared that his investment in Ladbroke had 'so involved his affairs as to compromise all of his property.' Some fortunes were made but many more were lost before the area we know today was completed. The Rev. Samuel Walker, for example, lost most of his investments in the Ladbroke and Portobello estates.

As we have seen earlier these estates were developed by Charles Henry Blake, son of a merchant mariner on the India route who became a planter in Bengal. Blake junior came to England already wealthy from the India estates and invested in property. And while Blake generally kept one step ahead of the game and the market, poor Walker, whose main ambition was to endow his parish of St Columb in Cornwall in such a fashion as to make it an episcopal home for the diocese, lost most of the money that Blake enticed from him. It was to end in disaster for Walker. In 1864 The *Building News* described the area around Arundel Gardens and Elgin Crescent as one of 'Naked carcases, crumbling decorations, fractured walls and slimy cement work'. The whole estate, it said, was 'a graveyard of buried hopes', and it was nicknamed 'The Stumps' and Ladbroke Gardens

became known as 'Goodwin Sands' or 'Coffin Row'.

Little patches of work proceeded but these were in the middle of deserted and dilapidated streets. In 1855, with spectacular debts mounting, Dr Walker handed over all his property to the management of trustees, including that part of the Portobello estate which was to become Colville Gardens and Powis Square. Things did not improve. As with much of the large terraced property in inner London, houses were divided and sub-divided into shabby tenements and rooms; in 1935 the locality in which Dr Walker had built his All Saints church was described as being 'largely a slum area turned into one-room tenements' and by the 1950s it was the centre of 'Rachmanism' and the exploitation of poor tenants. Only in recent times has the long climb back to desirability and respectability been successful.

Dr Walker died at the age of 59 in 1869 leaving a widow and young children and by then his inheritance of £250,000 had shrunk to £70,000. Blake, the most successful participant in the schemes, outlived him by three years, and Richard Roy became a respected Vestryman, Poor Law Guardian and Chairman of the Commissioners of the Kensington Improvement Act - he died in 1873. None, however, made a vast fortune from the venture which must have obsessed most of their lives, but they left a remarkable neighbourhood as their monument.

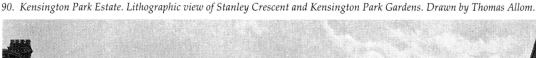

90. Kensington Park Estate. Lithographic view of Stanley Crescent and Kensington Park Gardens. Drawn by Thomas Allom.

91. *Ladbroke Grove, 1866.*

92. *View of eastern part of Ladbroke Road, showing nos 71-81 and 40-52, and an LCC fire engine station.*

93. Linden Lodge 1827, built by architect Thomas Allason who was also a resident. The extensive grounds included a lake, probably created from the gravel pits which had been on the site. (See p82.)

Prosperous Pembridge

The Ladbroke land also included the 28 acres which now consists of Pembridge and Chepstow Villas and their offshoots, and the western end of Westbourne Grove, but it was not until 1842 that a civil engineer, William Henry Jenkins, signed an agreement to develop them. The quality of the houses and their occupants was stipulated - there were to be no 'noisome trades'. Additionally, the Metropolitan Building Act of 1844 imposed new regulations on house building in London.

The Jenkins family had estates in Herefordshire and other parts of the border country as well as in Wales, and this accounts for much of the street naming in this area - Denbigh, Monmouth, Chepstow etc. Work and sales proceeded briskly and Jenkins was able to extend his development on to land owned by Robert Hall up to Portobello Road.

But the really grand development of this part of Notting Hill was proceeding on other land owned by Hall to the south, where two Devon-born brothers, Francis and William Radford, were constructing the houses which make up Pembridge Square and

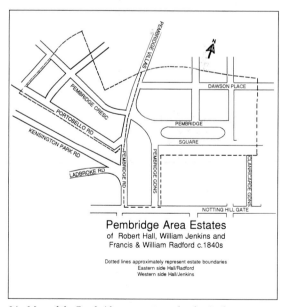

Pembridge Area Estates
of Robert Hall, William Jenkins and
Francis & William Radford c.1840s

Dotted lines approximately represent estate boundaries
Eastern side Hall/Radford
Western side Hall/Jenkins

94. Map of the Pembridge area estates, by the Author.

Dawson Place as well as a few more modest dwellings. This district then was commonly described as 'Bayswater', although still within the boundaries of Kensington, to add a touch of class to its standing. The Radfords built some 125 houses there before moving on even more ambitiously and successfully to Holland Park. When he died in 1900, Francis Radford left £260,000 and his funeral was attended by ten mourning coaches.

The Radfords had had the good sense to provide a mixed development, from the very grand (Pembridge Square) to the more homely terraces of Ledbury Road. The 1861 Census reveals that most of the households in Pembridge Gardens had at least three servants, and the occupants included merchants, stockbrokers, surveyors and a colliery owner; in Pembridge Square the number of servants quite often exceeded that of the family itself, with not only a cook, butler and lady's maid, but a footman and page.

In contrast to all this, development taking place in the north-west of the estate at Westbourne Grove was of mixed quality by a variety of builders, begun in the mid 1840s and not completed for about twenty years. Very little survives, indication enough of its inferior quality. Westbourne Grove (then called Archer Street) was the shopping centre for that area and for the servants of the Pembridge villas. Traders included tailors, milliners, dressmakers, a hairdresser, French dyer, a bonnet and stay warehouse and a clockmaker. G. Appleford's 'Cowkeeper and dairy'

suggests that the country was still not so far away.

The third and smallest of Ladbroke's Notting Hill holdings was the five acre plot now occupied by Linden Gardens, and this was actually the first to be built upon soon after 1822. Here, Allason built himself a house, Linden Lodge, on the west side of the road, with two acres of gardens, including a lake, stables and a gardener's cottage. Other residents of this delightful backwater, protected from the noisy high street by the erection of ornamental gates and a lodge house (now 24b Notting Hill Gate), included the artists William Mulready (who designed the first penny postage envelope for Rowland Hill), and Thomas Creswick, both of whom recorded scenes of the area at this time.

In 1849 Felix Ladbroke, son of Richard Weller Ladbroke, sold the freehold of this plot to Allason, and on *his* death it passed to one of his four daughters, Louisa, and her husband, Arthur Bull. The coming of the railway in 1868 encouraged them to capitalise on their inheritance. Their son, Sir William Bull, MP, writing his 'Recollections of Bayswater 50 years Ago' in the *Bayswater Chronicle* in 1923, said: 'They pulled down the old house [Linden Lodge], filled up the lake and built Linden Gardens and the shops in front, on the site of the house, meadows and gardens. The Metropolitan Railway paid a considerable sum for permission to run under the estate.'

All that remained were eight paired houses on the east side, dwarfed by the high terraces all around them.

95. *No. 42 Linden Gardens, 1970, one of the few original houses in the road to survive.*

96. *Pembridge Road near Notting Hill Gate c1900.*

97. *Archer Street, renamed Westbourne Grove in 1938, was a popular shopping centre for the domestics of the Pembridge villas.*

98. The Tile Kiln 1824.

The Piggeries

By 1781 some 17 acres of clay land north of 'the road to Uxbridge' were being used as brickfields. The first person to make his home in this desolate place is said to have been a chimney sweep and scavenger called Samuel Lake, who had been turned out of his premises in Tottenham Court Road, and who was later joined by a friend called Stephens, a bow-string maker. Pig keeping was added to their activities.

At about the same time other pig-keepers, displaced from their smallholdings in what is now the Connaught Square area of Paddington, as the Bishop of London developed his estate, also settled in the Notting Hill bricklands. There were no building restrictions, no sanitary regulations and, indeed, no drainage. Hovels, sheds and huts were the main feature of this squalid area, which stank of pigs and pig swill. By 1840 the colony consisted of two streets and side alleys, all within an area now bounded by Darnley Terrace to the north and Treadgold Street on the south (a single kiln still stands as an ancient monument in Walmer Road).

The pigs far outnumbered the human inhabitants. In 1849 it was estimated that there were 3,000 pigs and 1,000 residents in an area of eight or nine acres. And in the middle was a pool of fetid water known as 'the Ocean'. It was hardly surprising that the death rate among children in the area was 87 per cent in 1856.

The Piggeries were far from the sight and concern of the Vestry and its duties were taken up by charities, both religious and secular. But it was Kensington's first Medical Officer of Health, Dr Francis Godrich, who was given the formidable task of cleaning up the area. Opposition was fierce from the pig-keepers themselves and, perversely, the Vestry did not want them to lose the pigs and therefore their livelihoods because they could then become a charge on the poor rate. However, the number of pigs was gradually reduced but it was not until the 1890s that the last pig snuffled away. In any case, the population found it more rewarding to take in laundry than to keep pigs.

In the 1860s the brickmakers and pig-keepers were joined by a gipsy colony of forty to fifty vehicles, and it was their 'King', a temperance convert called Hearn, who began evangelising among the gipsy families, a mission

99. Cottages in the Kensington Potteries, 1855. From Ragged Homes and How to Mend Them, *by Mrs M. Bayly.*

100. Houses in Walmer Road. Drawing by W. Cleverley Alexander.

continued later by the famous 'Gipsy Smith'.

In 1889 the Rev. C.E. Roberts of St Clement's church and the Rev. Dr Thornton of St John's, appealed in a letter to *The Times* for an open space for the children of Notting Hill. As a result the old brickfield and the area of 'the Ocean', previously earmarked as a site for a waste destructor, became instead the nucleus of Avondale Park, opened in 1892, and named in memory of the recently deceased Duke of Clarence and Avondale.

It was only a year after the park was opened that the *Daily News* described the area adjacent as 'Avernus' (Lake Avernus - the fabled entrance to hell). Almost all the houses in streets like Sirdar Road and Wilsham Street were massively over-occupied or else were the most primitive of lodging houses in which a bed on the floor cost a few pennies a night. By 1904 new low-cost tenements were being built, such as Seymour King's Buildings (named after the first mayor of the new Royal Borough of Kensington, who had made an interest-free loan to the council for their construction). The Improved Tenements Association bought 64-year leases of four houses in Walmer Road in 1900, and these were modernised and divided into two-room tenements to accommodate thirteen families for rents of five shillings a week. There were still problems. One tenant was said to be a 'terror to his neighbours', and was evicted after keeping pigeons and ripping out the basement to make pigeon houses.

Another housing association, the Wilsham Trust, was formed by Ladies-in-Waiting at Kensington Palace (then the residence of Queen Victoria's daughters, Princess Louise and Princess Beatrice) and in 1920 this and the Improved Tenements Association amalgamated to form the Rowe Housing Trust. From the turn of the century housing charities in Notting Hill proliferated and by the 1930s the Kensington Housing Trust, the Sutton Dwellings Trust and the Peabody Trust between them had built almost twice as many new homes as had the borough council.

Generally speaking, Kensington Council, which has been Conservative since its formation, has been an unenthusiastic supporter of municipal housing (only two wards, Golborne and Norland, usually elect Labour members). But there have been exceptions on the Tory benches. Lord Balfour of Burleigh, was a pioneer of Council housing. It was he who founded the Kensington Housing Trust after protests about the housing of railway workers living in Great Western Road, and he continued his campaigns up to his death in 1967. Another Conservative reformer, Henry Dickens, a grandson of the novelist, was often at odds with his own party - Henry Dickens Court, on the site of the notorious Crescent Street, is named after him as the Balfour of Burleigh estate commemorates Lord Balfour. Robert Jenkins, whose father had been a Church Street grocer, was a zealous campaigner for public health and infant and maternity welfare; he later became Conservative MP for Dulwich.

There were women too on the majority benches who showed their concern beyond the southern wards in which

Life in the avernus

Life in the avernus of Notting Dale, the area around Pottery Lane and surrounding streets at the turn of the century. A few gipsies still lingered with their vans and tinkers yards, children often depended on charity soup kitchens for their one hot meal of the day and old men, dying of consumption, sat out on chairs at their doors. Pictures by H. Robinson from "The Strand Magazine."

101. *Life in the Avernus of Notting Dale.*

102. *The rent collector calls in the Blechynden Road area.*

103. *Latimer Road Mission - feeding hungry children.*

104. *Kenley Street before construction of workmen's flats, 1904.*

102

105. *Advert for S. Pomeroy, 134 Lancaster Road, hosiers and hatters, in 1909.*

they were normally elected. These included Lady Pepler and Lady Petrie, both to serve later on the LCC, and Sybil Kerslake, whose interest lay in youth work, particularly among the large Jewish community.

It is an interesting commentary on the change in local politics that in the first four decades of this century that in the London boroughs which replaced the old vestries, the representatives of the right were by and large people of trade - grocers, builders and estate agents etc, while those on the left included such trade unionists as Walter Little and Fred Burns. Today, both parties draw most often on the professions, such as lawyers, accountants and insurance executives.

When parliamentary boundary changes came into force in 1974 Kensington (North) ceased to be a separate constituency, being absorbed into the northern half of Kensington (South) to form the new Kensington constituency

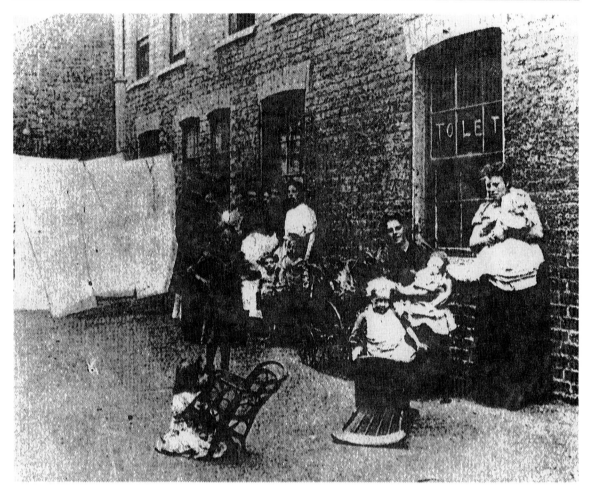

106. *A scene in the Potteries*

(the southern half joined Chelsea). This marked the end of Labour's hold on the Notting Hill area which it had enjoyed since 1945.

107. *Kenley Street 1970.*

The Clockmaker and the Colonel

The area north of Holland Park Avenue, which now includes Norland Square, St James's Gardens and Royal Crescent, might well have been the home of a large lunatic asylum had not its 19th-century owner demanded too high a price for its 52 acres. By 1784 it was in the possession of the famous clockmaker, Benjamin Vulliamy, who lived in a large house on the site of the present No. 130 Holland Park Avenue. The house burned down in 1825 and two years later its ruins and the land around it were offered to the Middlesex Justices of the Peace who were looking for a site for a new county lunatic asylum. Vulliamy, however, wanted too much, and the Justices instead bought a site at Hanwell.

In the grounds of Vulliamy's house was a well, said to have been the first of its kind to be constructed in England. It consisted of a shaft four feet in diameter, sunk to a depth of 236 feet, with a further 30 feet of narrow boring which brought up water from the underlying gravel at a rate of 46 gallons a minute. In his *History of Kensington*, Faulkner describes it as 'Vulliamy's overflowing well'. It was said to be specially good for washing and a little water company was set up by two entrepreneurs who called

themselves the Notting Hill Water Works to sell the water to the general public at two shillings and sixpence a ton or a halfpenny a pail. The well was finally covered in 1840.

The estate was later purchased by a City lawyer, Charles Richardson, who planned an up-market arrangement of crescents and squares. He committed himself to enormous capital outlay and by 1844 his total liabilities amounted to about £45,000, much of this being used for loans to builders. One of the biggest investors in the estate was Charles Stewart, the MP for Penryn, who took building leases for 43 plots in Royal Crescent and many more in St Ann's Villas, Holland Park Avenue, Queensdale Road and Norland Square. The gracious proportions of the Crescent, and the width of Addison Avenue leading up to St James's Gardens, owe their design not only to the taste of their architect, Robert Cantwell (who also worked extensively in Ladbroke), but also to the practical demands of sewerage installation.

The Census for 1851 shows that all the large houses in these new streets were in single-family occupation with a large number of servants (who formed a third of the population). Norland Square had a number of doctors and lawyers, a Russian diplomat, an American author with seven servants, a naval captain and a quarry owner; Royal Crescent could boast three lawyers, two clergymen and three stockbrokers; while Addison Avenue had army officers and a surgeon at the best end but at the southern end, where the

108. *'View of Royal Crescent, Norland Estate, Notting Hill'. The spire in the background was intended to grace the church of St James's, but it never materialised.*

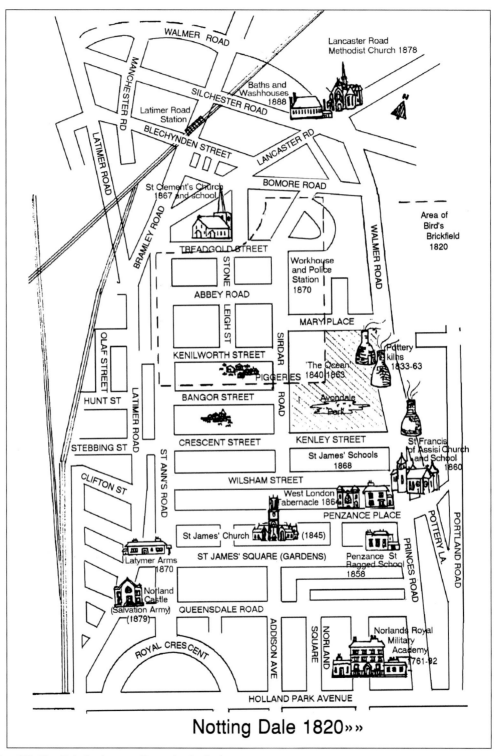

109. *Map of Notting Dale development. Drawn by the Author.*

110. *Norland Square, c1904*

111. *The junction of Holland Park Avenue and Norland Square*

houses were smaller, there was a horse dealer, a gunmaker and an omnibus proprietor.

But the housing market was sluggish and Richardson had to sell part of his land, a brickfield to the north, to one of his tenants, William Morrison, who proceeded to run up cheap and small houses to form the Wilsham Street area. This explains the sudden transition of style and quality of houses a short distance north of Royal Crescent. Richardson had obviously foreseen what the mean development adjacent would be like, for he stipulated that there should be no way connecting his own streets to Morrison's, especially to that 'notorious place of ill fame, Notting Dale'. Richardson later went bankrupt and in later life earned his living selling patent medicines in Glasgow.

112. *St Quintin Estate map, drawn by the Author.*

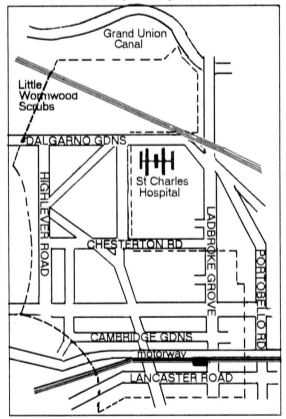

St Quintin Estate

Dotted lines approximately
represent estate boundaries

113. *The design for St James's Square (now Gardens) c1847 by the architect, John Barnett, who was responsible for 37 three-storey houses here.*

THE COLONEL'S SUBURB

Colonel Matthew Chitty Downes St Quintin, a former colonel in the 17th Lancers, came from a family which owned extensive estates in Yorkshire, and in 1859 he inherited the Notting Barns farmlands from his brother. The farm seems to have been a thriving one, at least up to the end of the 18th century, as its occupiers are recorded as having made generous gifts to the parish church. In 1860 its fields covered 150 acres, with 'an ancient brick building surrounded by spacious barns and outhouses'. Even as late as 1873 residents took a country walk along its paths, bright with hawthorn and violets growing on the site of the Earl Percy pub in Ladbroke Grove. The farm house stood roughly at the junction of St Quintin Avenue and Chesterton Road, north of the Westway.

Colonel St Quintin, an absentee landlord, had no intention of becoming involved in building works. Instead he hired an architect to design some hand-

114. *A local trader. The billhead of R.N. Larter & Sons, 184 Holland Park Avenue in 1924. The invoice is for repairing a cracked lavatory basin and a faulty water tap, at a cost of 6/6d.*

some streets and leased sites to building speculators. Some four hundred houses were built on the St Quintin land between 1871-90 in such streets as Oxford and Cambridge Gardens, Highlever Road, Bassett Road, St Mark's Road, St Quintin Avenue and Maxilla Gardens (the latter largely destroyed by the motorway).

But even as late as 1922 there were pockets of open land. There were extensive grounds for cricket and tennis, and an athletics track on the land between St Quintin Avenue and the railway. It was on this land that the annual Notting Hill Flower and Home Improvement Show was held. This was to encourage poorer inhabitants to take a pride in their dwellings. Loftie's *History of London* (1888) speaks of a 'new quarter springing up rapidly upon the slope towards Kensal Green', the district being given the name of 'New Found Out'. Before St Quintin Avenue was formed the old athletics track was used by cavalry en route to exercise on Wormwood Scrubs, and a 'great stretch of common' between St Helen's Gardens and

115. Notting Barns Farm, c1830. Adapted by E. Woolmer from an older drawing.

Latimer Road was used to graze cattle. The space between the two railway lines became a desolate no-man's land across which a stream ran in a brick culvert. This was also the site of a shooting range where a gunsmith allowed his customers to try out their weapons by firing at an iron stag on rails.

Old tales still live on about this more distant corner of North Kensington which, for a brief period between the wars, had the veneer if not the architecture of a Betjeman suburb, with tennis and bowling clubs, and a thriving British Legion branch.

One tale is a ghost story. In June 1934 a young motorist was killed early one morning at the junction of Chesterton Road and Cambridge Gardens when his car mysteriously swerved off the road and hit a lamppost. At the inquest it was suggested that the reason for the accident was that he had swerved to avoid a ghost bus, a No. 7, operated by the General Omnibus Company (though London Transport then ran the buses). There had been various sightings of the vehicle, usually at 1.15am, going at great speed down the centre of the road.

116. No. 12. St Ann's Villas

117. Coronation tea in Bangor Street in 1937.

118. The North Pole in North Pole Road, c1910.

119. Bangor Street being demolished in the 1950s.

120. *Portland Road in the 1940s.*

On Stage

When it opened in November 1898 the Coronet Theatre at Notting Hill Gate was described in *The Era* as a 'theatre of which the whole country may be proud'. Just over twenty years later it had succumbed to the new craze for 'moving pictures', and by the 1970s it was fighting for its life, even as a cinema. That battle was happily successful, but only after a local voluntary effort. The Coronet still stands, if somewhat shabby, on the corner of Uxbridge Street.

It was built for the impresario, Edward George Saunders, to designs by W.G.R. Sprague, with a seating capacity of over 1100. Handsomely decorated in traditional gilt and red plush, it boasted six boxes, with a grandly named crush bar in the present foyer, and had gilt figures on the copper faced cupola which crowns the roof.

The first production - *The Geisha* - opened before the building was complete and resulted in Saunders being prosecuted, as the LCC had not yet granted it a licence, but presumably the publicity made it worth while to him. During its 18 years as a live theatre the Coronet stage was graced by many famous actors, including Sarah Bernhardt (old, and with one leg amputated by then), Henry Irving, Martin Harvey and Mrs Patrick Campbell.

The name Coronet survived long after it became a cinema in 1921, but it was changed for a time to the Gaumont in 1950.

In the mid-19th century a hall in Archer Street (now Westbourne Grove), which had been used by non-conformists, was opened as the Victoria Hall Theatre and later (in 1866) renamed The Bijou, when it was used by touring companies and as a music hall -. Albert Chevalier is said to have made his debut there. The auditorium was on the first floor of a dwelling house and therefore had a complex exit system. It was the only theatre in Britain that was licensed for public performances with the proviso that all the furnishings in it had to be made of wool as a fire precaution. From 1911 to 1918 The Bijou was used as a cinema, but in 1920 became the headquar-

121. The Coronet Theatre in Edwardian times

CORONET THEATRE.

| Lessees | - | - | JOHN HALPIN LTD. |
| Managing Director | - | | Mr. JOHN HALPIN. |

MONDAY, OCTOBER 23rd, 1911, for Six Nights at 8.
TWO MATINEES: Wednesday and Saturday, at 2.30.

Mrs. LANGTRY
(LADY DE BATHE),

Supported by her Powerful West-End Company, in

" THE DEGENERATES,"

A Comedy in Four Acts, by SYDNEY GRUNDY.

Characters :

Duke of Orme ...	...	...	Mr. HUBERT HARBEN
Sir William Samaurez, Bart.	...	...	... Mr. PHILIP DARIEN
Isidore de Lorano	...	...	Mr. ALFRED MANSFIELD
Viscount Stornoway	...	...	... Mr. FRED PENLEY
Mr. Carl Hentsch	...	...	... Mr. ENTWISTLE
Mr. Marcus Mosenthal	...	...	Mr. ROBERT RIVERS
Saunders	...	...	Mr. DICK ECKERSLEY
A Butler	...	...	... Mr. HORTON TREE
Pedro	...	...	Mr. WILLIAM RICHMON
A Footman	...	...	Mr. WILLIAM GARRETT
Mrs. Trevelyan	...	...	... **Mrs. LANGTRY**
			(Lady de Bathe)
Lady Saumarez	...	...	Miss VIOLET MACAREE
Hon. Mrs. Bennett Bolder	...	...	Miss LEONORA BRAHAM
Lady Stornoway	...	...	Miss WINIFRED WILLIS
Una Trevelyan	...	...	... Miss SYBIL WALSH

Act 1	-	-	-	At Sir William Saumarez's (evening)
Act 2	-	-	-	At Mrs. Trevelyan's (the next evening)
Act 3	-	-	-	At Mr. De Lorano's (the same night)
Act 4	-	-	-	At Mrs. Trevelyan's (the next morning)

The Dresses worn by LADY de BATHE have been specially designed for this Play by
Paquin, of Paris and Dover Street, London.

At 8 o'clock (not Matinees),

" 'TWIXT NIGHTFALL AND THE LIGHT."

Captain James Beaufoy	...	...	... Mr. ALFRED MANSFIELD
Margery (his Wife)	...	...	Miss SYBIL WALSH
Arnold Chaloner	...	...	Mr. FRED PENLEY

Scene—The Beaufoy's House, near Pretoria. Present Day.

| Business Manager | ... | For | Mr. NORMAN G. APPLEBY |
| Stage Manager | ... | Mrs. LANGTRY | Mr. FRED PENLEY |

122. *From a 1911 Coronet programme for* The Degenerates *in which Lily Langtry appeared.*

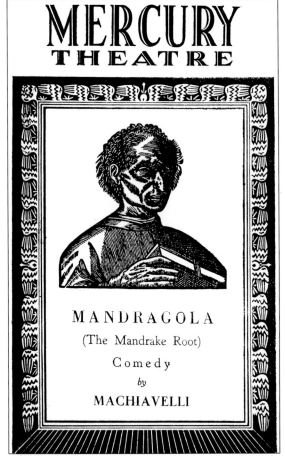

MERCURY THEATRE

MANDRAGOLA
(The Mandrake Root)

Comedy

by

MACHIAVELLI

123. *A 1949 Mercury Theatre programme for The* Mandragola, *a comedy by Machiavelli*

ters of a distinguished repertory company formed by Lena Ashwell. Later, renamed the Twentieth Century Theatre, it was used by amateur companies as well as for public and political meetings. In 1963 the fittings were stripped out and the interior converted into a warehouse for antique furniture.

Although purpose-built as a cinema in 1905, the Electric Cinema in Portobello Road (believed to be the second earliest in London) was later used as a music hall, the Imperial Playhouse. It is now the Electric Cinema Club and is much revered by serious cinema enthusiasts for its showing of classic films.

The Mercury Theatre building in Ladbroke Road began in 1851 as a Congregational Sunday School attached to Horbury Chapel (now Kensington Temple). After the 1st World War it became the headquarters of Madame (later Dame) Marie Rambert's Russian School of Dancing and in the 1930s she opened her own Ballet Club company with an experimental season. This was followed by the famous series of Sunday evening performances in which the artistes included many dancers later to become stars

such as Robert Helpmann, and choreographers Frederick Ashton and Walter Gore. Among the ballets first seen there was the popular *Lady into Fox*. The Ballet club was disbanded in 1940 but out of it was born the Ballet Rambert Company. Parallel activities in the straight theatre were run in the same building by Madame Rambert's husband, Ashley Dukes, and in 1935 the Mercury, as it was called, gained national attention with the first performance of the T.S. Eliot play, *Murder in the Cathedral*. Christopher Fry's *The Lady's Not for Burning* and *A Phoenix Too Frequent* also made their debuts there. The building was converted into a private dwelling when the ballet company moved to new premises in the 1980s.

The popularity of Club theatre in the late 1940s and early 1950s (the forerunner of today's fringe theatre in pubs) saw a rash of new theatres in Kensington, but especially in Notting Hill. The New Lindsey Theatre was established in the Lindsey Hall in the Mall in the late 1940s and this could claim to be a pioneer in the theatre club movement; its director, Peter Cotes, went on to even greater successes at the New Boltons Theatre Club in South Kensington. The New Lindsey came late into the limelight when Queen Mary attended a performance of the 'banned' play, *Pick Up Girl*, by Elsa Shelley, on her 78th birthday. The theatre enjoyed another spell of fame under Robert Henderson, when its productions included such then unknown actors as Kenneth More, Dirk Bogarde and Jean Kent.

In her flat in Brunswick House, a block of flats above shops on the corner of the Mall and Notting Hill Gate, next door to the New Lindsey, Bertha N. Graham tried to keep alive the flickering flame of the 1930 Players in post-war days. Elderly and rather deaf, and supported by her friend and secretary, the devoted 'Miss Henry', Miss Graham reigned over little gatherings at which she would recall past West End successes and attempt to continue the Players with plays, readings and recitals in her home.

The Chepstow Theatre Club was also located in a private house. Once known as The Gateway, it was in a converted basement room at the rear of one of the houses in Chepstow Villas. First used for straight plays, its last productions in the late 1950s were revues. Another Gateway existed for a few years in the 1950s in Westbourne Grove, mainly presenting late-night revues, although it enjoyed some success in 1951 with a transfer of *Journey's End* to the Westminster Theatre, and a production of *A Sting in the Tail* by Tom Purefoy.

In more recent times Notting Hill Gate's reputation for theatrical enterprise has been kept alive by the Gate Theatre, situated above the Prince Albert in Pembridge Road. In 1992 it won the first prize in the London Weekend Television 'Plays on Stage' competition for *Bohemian Lights* by Ramon del Valle-Inclan.

MERCURY THEATRE

THE MERCURY AND PILGRIM PLAYERS (Administrator: Ireland Cutter)

in association with the Arts Council of Great Britain

SECOND SEASON OF NEW PLAYS BY POETS

presented by E. Martin Browne

MURDER IN THE CATHEDRAL

by T. S. ELIOT

décor by Stella Mary Pearce

Produced by E. Martin Browne

124. Mercury Theatre programme 1947 for a production of Murder in the Cathedral *by T.S. Eliot.*

A Bad Start for Golborne

In 1865 an interesting '*Plan for the Laying out of the Portobello Estate for Building Purposes*' was drawn up by Henry Currey, the architect who was the designer of St Thomas's Hospital, and who was already involved in work in the St Quintin area. The names 'Green Lane Park' or 'Portobello Park' were proposed for the new district and the intention was to bridge the canal and railway to link Golborne Road with Harrow Road, but this was superseded by the Paddington Canal Company's decision to build a toll footbridge in open land at what was to become Wedlake Street, known as the 'Halfpenny Steps'. As it was, Currey's ambitious plan never materialised and it was the notable - or perhaps by now, notorious - Charles Henry Blake, who acquired 130 acres of the estate in 1863. Soon scores of builders were at work building long, drab streets, such as Golborne and Acklam Roads, in terraces of narrow three-storey houses on plots so shallow that there was room only for a very small back yard. The agent for Colonel St Quintin, who was engaged in development to the west of Ladbroke Grove, was so worried by the standard of housing on Blake's land that he threatened to prevent access to it unless arrangements were made to regulate the class of houses to be built there.

Nevertheless, this sub-standard development forged ahead and by 1879 practically the whole triangle bounded by Ladbroke Grove, Harrow Road and the Metropolitan Railway was full of dwellings that were already degenerating into slums, although Blake's stated intention had been to attract middle-class residents.

The same applied north of the GWR railway line in Southam Street, Edenham Street, Hazlewood Crescent and Bosworth Road which, by the turn of the century, was described as being one of the worst districts in London. In Southam Street 2,500 people lived in 140 nine-room houses with minimal toilet facilities.

Large-scale slum clearance did not begin until 1933 when the borough council closed unfit basements and started improving conditions in the houses. By 1938 a hundred new flats had been built, mainly by the Kensington Housing Trust, plus over sixty more by the Gas Light & Coke Company, whose innovative flats at Kensal House were intended as a practical experiment in equipping blocks with gas fuelled apparatus. Rents were low, and there were communal facilities such as nurseries and laundries. After the Second World War, the whole 20 acres between Bosworth Road and Great Western Road were redeveloped by the borough council and the LCC, mainly with unacceptable tower blocks where improved sanitation has not compensated for social deprivation, and new problems have replaced those of the past. Graffiti-defaced and grimy concrete walkways are no less depressing or dangerous than were the streets with their teeming life, children playing in the gutters, and old people gossiping in doorways.

Golborne Road had its shabby shops and the Golborne Road Free Church ran a hostel for down-and-outs in the 1950s and '60s where the 'Tin Hat Pastor', the Rev. Bertrand Peake, preached fiery sermons. He gained his nickname from a wartime ministry in Fulham. A colourful character, the legends which accompanied him included an episode when one of the parties in a domestic dispute confiscated the instruments of the children's band. Here, too, was Godfrey Clarke and his sister in the corn chandler's shop that their parents opened in 1883; Godfrey had a passion for cats and the theatre. From the First World War to the outbreak of the Second the 'Cobbler Poet', Henry Burns, lived here; he posted up a 'Poem for the Day' in his shop window among the boot polish, leather soap and Goddard's Liniment. Two volumes of his poetry survive; the first, published in 1913, price 6d, contained poems on earlier events such as the Boer War, the second, in 1919, one shilling, is described as having 'thrilling and dramatic poems including many ballads of the First World War'. An ardent Socialist, he lived to see his son, Fred Burns, become one of the first Labour councillors, and later an alderman of the Royal Borough of Kensington.

125. Southam Street in the 1960s.

Read All About It

A VANISHED PAPER
In 1853, Charles James Strutt, a jobbing printer who had set up business in a terrace of shops at the southern end of Church Street, decided to publish a local newspaper. The government tax on newspapers, which he described as a 'tax on knowledge', had just been lifted, and the first issue of the *Kensington Gazette* appeared as a four-page tabloid, approximately 12" x 9". The contents included not only local but national events, such as the Crimean War, and Strutt, as its editor as well as its publisher, had strong views on all subjects. A free churchman and a keen supporter of Temperance, his opinions did not prevent him from accepting advertisements for brandy and gin at a shilling a pint. He was also a poet and rarely missed an opportunity to commemorate events in verse.

The newspaper, at first a freesheet supported by its advertisers, later cost a penny as it increased in size and scope. It lasted for two years, then disappeared as Mr Strutt, it seems, moved to Holborn where he began a new career in what would be known today as public relations journalism. Over a century later his daughter, Edith Strutt, then in her nineties, arrived at the office of the *Kensington News* in Church Street, carrying the only existing bound copy of the hundred or so issues of the *Gazette,* wrapped in brown paper. The old lady, then living alone in a room in Kentish Town, feared that this, and some originals of her father's poems, would probably be thrown away when she died and she asked the editor to accept them as a gift for posterity. There is no record of the *Gazette* in the British Library Newspaper Collection but these editions, which have been microfilmed, may be seen at Kensington Central Library.

The *Gazette*, appearing as it did at the time that Notting Hill was changing from a rural to an urban neighbourhood, provides an invaluable reference for the events and views of the time.

THE KENSINGTON NEWS
It is generally supposed that James Wakeham, who founded the *Kensington News* and *West London Times* in 1869, was apprenticed to Charles Strutt. Certainly it was in 1854, the year that Strutt decided to leave Kensington, that Wakeham set up his own business at No. 4 Bedford Terrace (later No. 118 Kensington Church Street). He and his family lived in the rooms above the shop, where for the first years he was a jobbing printer. In 1865 Wakeham began his first publishing venture, the *Kensington and Chelsea News*

126. *James Wakeham, who founded the* Kensington News *in 1869.*

which in 1869 was dropped in favour of the *Kensington News and West London Times*. By then he was one of the largest printers in London with over forty hand-setting compositors employed in various premises; his printing contracts included government and vestry work. His early machines were steam-driven, the printing being carried out in the basement until the neighbours complained about the noise and vibration, and then a larger works was leased at Rabbit Row at the northern end of Church Street, where a gas engine was installed.

Wakeham died in 1885, to be succeeded by his son, also James, who himself died at the early age of 46. The family had already suffered a tragedy in 1878, when his sister, Harriet Fanny, and her fiancé, were drowned when the excursion steamer, *The Princess Alice,* sank in the Thames Estuary with the loss of 700 lives.

When the old firm became a limited company in 1901 the directors installed one of the first Lanston Monotype machines. Again the neighbours complained and the equipment had to be moved to another part of the building. Also, in 1902 two wall telephones, known as 'constant message machines', were rented from the Postmaster General. The company that year dispensed with their delivery horse

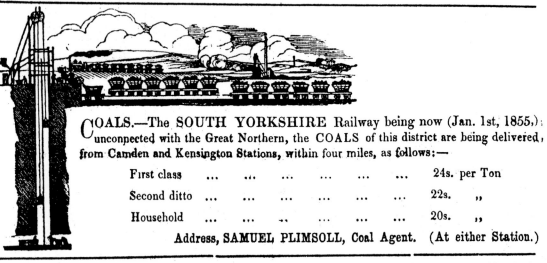

INCE HALL COAL AND CANNEL COMPANY,

Deliver direct from their Collieries in Lancashire,
for ready money only.

Best Wallsend Coal	26	0
Best Seconds do.	25	0
Cannel for Drawing Rooms..............		
Cannel for Gas Purposes		
Steam Coal for Brewers, Bakers, }		
Distillers, and others................		

𝕮𝔥𝔦𝔢𝔣 𝕺𝔣𝔣𝔦𝔠𝔢.—West London Railway Station, Kensington.

LEE & JERDEIN.

VIEW OF CANNEL & WALLSEND COAL PITS.

COALS.—The SOUTH YORKSHIRE Railway being now (Jan. 1st, 1855,) unconnected with the Great Northern, the COALS of this district are being delivered, from Camden and Kensington Stations, within four miles, as follows:—

First class	...	...	...	...	...	...	24s. per Ton
Second ditto	...	...	...	...	...	...	22s. ,,
Household	...	...	...	...	...	...	20s. ,,

Address, SAMUEL PLIMSOLL, Coal Agent. (At either Station.)

COALS, 22s. per Ton ; Best Inland 24s. ; Best Walls End, 28s. COKE, 16s. per Chaldron.
Address, JOHN WOODWARD, 33, HIGH STREET, KENSINGTON.

And at the Great Northern Coal Office, Knightsbridge.

TO PHOTOGRAPHISTS.—PREPARED COLLODION for PHOTOGRAPHIC PURPOSES, Instantaneous ditto; Iodizing Solution; Glacial Acetic, Gallic and Pyrogallic Acids; Nitrate of Silver; Cyanuret of Potassium, and every preparation required for Photographic Practice, may be obtained of

JOHN ROSSITER,
OPERATIVE AND PHOTOGRAPHIC CHEMIST,

☞ A LIST SENT ON APPLICATION.   *1, Lonsdale-place, Notting hill, near Pembridge villas.*

POTICHOMANIA or the ART of DECORATING GLASS to IMITATE CHINA. The necessary materials for this fashionable work, at the lowest possible price, may be had at

The Misses Butchers' Ornamental Needlework · Repository ; No. 7, Grove terrace, Notting hill,
Opposite Lord Holland's Park.

127. Advertisements from the Kensington Gazette *in June 1855.*

128. *Offices of the* Kensington News *in Kensington Church Street decorated for the Queen's Jubilee in 1897.*

and cart, selling them to their own driver for £15 on the understanding that it had first claim on his services on Fridays and Saturdays for distribution of the paper. It was also decided to supply delivery boys with mackintosh capes. These boys, who bought the paper wholesale for a halfpenny and sold it for a penny, were described as urchins who invested their all in speculation - often forming themselves into a company. 'One family of five, the youngest only five years old, commenced with a capital of 3d and, astonishing as it may appear, cleared sufficient to provide themselves with a Sunday dinner.'

Management of the business passed to a cousin of Wakeham's, William Hill, and an executor, Henry Manfield, whose son, Harry, was still managing director of the *Kensington News* when it was bought by the North West London Press in 1965. Much involved in the management of the paper after the Second World War was Marjorie Thom, a daughter of a North Kensington builder, who together with her husband fostered the 'Brighter Kensington and Chelsea' garden scheme, which the paper sponsored for many years.

During the Second World War the *News*, in common with other papers, was much reduced in size, but despite nearby bombs did not miss an issue.. It was in this period that the present author first worked

for it and later became its editor until 1972, when the paper was merged into the London Newspaper Group together with seven other west London newspapers. The *News* was the first to draw attention in the mid 1950s to the activities of the rent racketeer, Perc Rachman.

The *Kensington News* was the starting point for a number of celebrated writers. These include the critic, Barry Norman, Alan Franks of *The Times*, John Picton of the *Toronto Star*, Gavin Weightman, John Wright and the well-known South Coast journalist, Adam Trimingham.

The Church Street premises closed in 1972 .

BOOKS FOR A READING PUBLIC

Lord Stanley, son of the old Conservative Earl of Derby, made a speech in 1855 in which he listed the institutions and public works which no well-ordered town of magnitude should be without: '...a place of worship, a school for children between the age of five and fifteen, a public park and a free, rate-supported library...'

The Public Libraries Acts, the first of which had been passed by Parliament in the early 1850s, applied only to parishes with more than 10,000 inhabitants and its local adoption also required the consent of two thirds of the ratepayers. The library rate was

129. Notting Hill (North Kensington) Library, a postcard c1904.

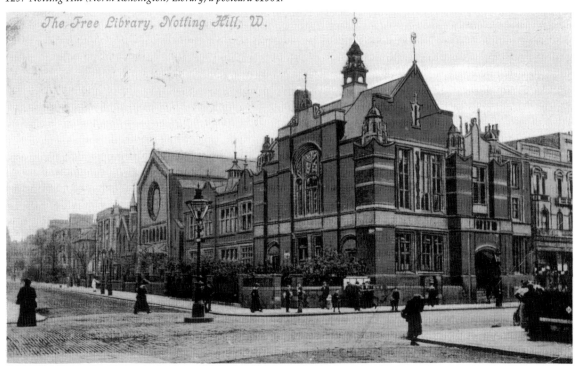

limited to a halfpenny in the £ and could not be used to provide books, the libraries having to rely on gifts to fill their shelves. In Kensington even such a modest expenditure as this was rigorously opposed by the Vestry, despite the efforts of one wealthy resident, the Manchester banker and MP, James Heywood, who came to live in Kensington Palace Gardens in 1858 and was a champion of adult education.

A few years earlier a Parochial Institute had been set up in Kensington with the object of providing working-class men and women with evening classes, lectures and a library reading room. The library was sparsely stocked through a subscription to the commercial Churston's Library which, for £16 a year, allowed 100 books to be selected from their catalogue. The Institute's fees were high in relation to the general cost of living (the cost of attending a lecture could be as much as half a pint of gin) and physical conditions were miserable, with meetings usually in unheated schoolrooms.

In 1874 James Heywood, unable despite all his efforts to persuade the Vestry to adopt the Public Libraries Act, decided to finance a library himself. Premises were found in a former shop at 106 Notting Hill Gate, a site now occupied by Campden Hill Towers, and the library opened its doors on 15 August that year. When the Public Libraries Act was eventually adopted by the Vestry in June 1887 Heywood offered his own library stock as a free gift to the newly-appointed Commissioners for Public Libraries and Museums, and after a brief closure the old library reopened in January 1888 as Kensington's first publicly-owned free library.

The Librarian of this new establishment, a Miss Isabella Stamp, had as her assistant a young man called Herbert Jones, of Irish birth despite his Welsh name, and it was he who was appointed Kensington's first Chief Librarian, a post he held until 1924. He was the first municipal librarian in London to recognise the value of a local topographical collection and today's local studies collection in the borough owes a lot to his enthusiasm and skill.

North Kensington library opened in 1891 in Ladbroke Grove - it was the first purpose-built library in the borough and the only one of the early buildings still in use as such, although the library erected in Kensal Town survived to be passed over to Paddington (now Westminster) when the boundaries changed at the turn of the century.

Despite local opposition, a children's room was opened in the basement of this library in 1912 and since that time the children's service has developed out of all recognition, with full programmes of storytelling, book weeks and films.

It was not until 1926 that direct access to the library shelves was allowed; before that books had to be

130. Poster advertising a public meeting to discuss the proposal for a free library in Kensal Town.

selected from the catalogue, so no browsing was possible. Rules were strict, conversation being restricted to the merest whisper.

In 1949 a surface air raid shelter in Bulmer Mews was converted into a library to serve Notting Hill Gate and continued until 1955 when it was replaced by the branch library in Pembridge Square. There is also a Kensal branch in Golborne Road.

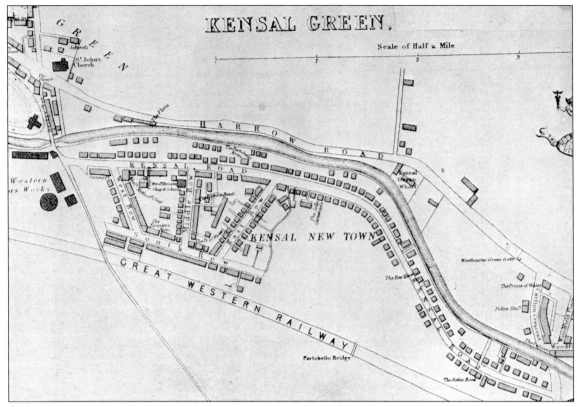

131. *Map of Kensal Green, from Edward Weller's* Weekly Dispatch Atlas, *1855-1860.*

Little Chelsea beyond Kensington

In the mid-19th century, William Kinnaird Jenkins, a lawyer, bought land in four fields which technically belonged to the parish of Chelsea, to create Kensal New Town. By 1850 four terraces of tiny cottage buildings, East Row, West Row, Middle Row and South Row, were in existence, together with the church of St John's, Kensal Green. The fact that the General Cemetery Company had bought 54 acres to the west for a new burial ground could not have been an attractive prospect at a time when adjacency to a cemetery was considered a drawback; in addition, land between the canal and the railway was being used to build a new works for the Western Gas Company.

Soon the houses of Kensal New Town were taken over by poor families, many of them Irish, engaged in laundry work or pig keeping. In their spare time they amused themselves with trotting races and dog breeding, the stock for the latter often the result of the Victorian crime of dog stealing. Bill George, a well-known prize fighter, was said to keep a Home for Dogs or 'Canine Castle', which was the first place to enquire for owners whose pets had gone missing.

Conditions deteriorated and Victorian do-gooders moved in. Missions, crèches, free clinics, workmen's clubs, temperance societies and day nurseries sprang up, but they were never really able to tackle the social and health problems. Nevertheless, in 1902 Charles Booth in his *Life and Labour of the London Poor* was able to say that the area 'retains something of the appearance of a village, trampled underfoot by the advance of London but able to show cottage gardens.'

The administration of this area by the parish of St Luke's, Chelsea was bound to be at a disadvantage and, given its poor population, Chelsea did little about it. There were also numerous disputes with Kensington as to responsibility for roads and pavements which fell near boundary lines. Despite this, Kensington was far from eager to accept responsibility for this pocket of population when London boroughs were reorganised at the beginning of this century.

132. *Backs of houses in East Row, Kensal Town. Drawing by W. Cleverley Alexander, 1911.*

133. *The Cottages, East Row. Watercolour drawing by W.E. Kell, 1911.*

134. An early drawing of The Plough, Kensal Green, a favourite place of the artist, George Morland. By Mary and Robert Banks.

135. A slum in Kensal Road, 1967.

Matters of Life and Death

An official report on conditions in Notting Dale in 1849 states 'The inhabitants all look unhealthy...with shrunken eyes and shrivelled skin, the women particularly complaining of sickness and want of appetite.' This was the year that the numbers of deaths from smallpox, diphtheria, typhoid and scarlet fever were added to by a cholera epidemic. Four years later cholera also claimed the Rev. E. Proctor Dennis, vicar of St John's in Ladbroke Grove.

Tuberculosis or 'consumption' was the cause of death of one person in six, more than all the other virulent infectious diseases, yet despite these alarming statistics Notting Hill and North Kensington had no hospital until the St Marylebone Infirmary - denied a new site within its own area - was built in St Charles' Square in 1881. Other than that there was a small Dispensary for out-patients opened in Church Street in 1849.

It is not surprising that publications such as Charles Strutt's *Kensington Gazette* contained plenty of advertising for patent medicines. People, rich and poor,

had only the quacks or apothecaries to rely on, and often the latter were better informed than the academic physicians who had little or no practical experience. During the 19th century surgeon-apothecaries became what are today general practitioners; as their reputation improved, people relied more on their diagnoses and prescriptions and were less inclined to use patent medicines or to prescribe themselves. But still it was possible to buy over the counter some quite powerful drugs - opium, for example, to reduce pain and a number of products which included it. Godfrey's Soothing Cordial, a medicine for babies, contained opium and was sold by the gallon - it was not banned until 1860, arousing great resentment among the poor who regarded this, together with the Temperance movement, as yet another impediment to the poor alleviating pain and misery.

There was no restriction on advertising by medical men, so Dr Hardinge of Albert Terrace, Notting Hill, 'near the turnpike', was able to take space in the *Gazette* in 1854 to announce that he was able to 'speedily and effectively cure not only rheumatism in all its forms, but epilepsy, hysteria and all nervous diseases such as scrofula ('King's Evil') and ulcerated legs.' He was one of the local doctors who gave free advice to the very poor, people who were also able to turn to the religious and philanthropic missions such as that which Miss ('Nurse') Thompson ran in Kensal Town in the 1890s.

136. The architect's drawing of the proposed St Marylebone Infirmary (later St Charles' Hospital)

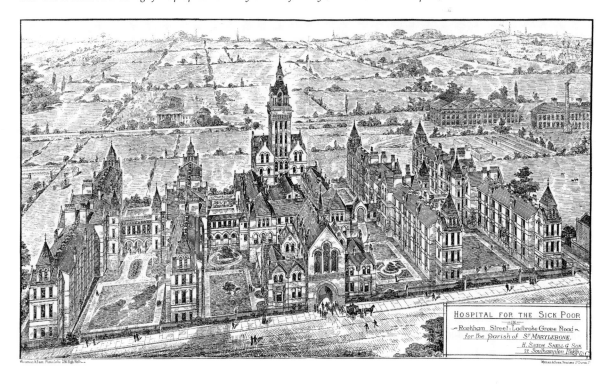

'Vaccination Gratis' was advertised in the first issue of the *Gazette* in 1853 at an Institute in Peel Street: 'perfect Vaccination to all classes of the community so that no person need be under obligation to the parish in respect thereof'. In 1855 the *Gazette* was recommending the appointment of Dr Ogier Ward, then the surgeon of the Kensington Dispensary, for the post of Medical Officer of Health for part of the parish. Dr Ward had recently published a report on the cholera epidemic in Wolverhampton, where he had been Secretary to the Board of Health.

In 1896 a ward was added to the Dispensary to accommodate eleven in-patients and its name was changed to the Dispensary and Children's Hospital. By the 1920s the project had vastly outgrown its premises. Princess Louise, Duchess of Argyll, who lived at Kensington Palace, instigated the formation of a local committee to establish a children's hospital in North Kensington. The foundation stone of the Princess Louise Hospital for Children was laid on the old War Memorial Playing Field site at St Quintin Avenue by the Princess herself. King George and Queen Mary agreed to open the hospital in May 1928 provided that it was free from debt and that the target was met by a fund which included a scheme to collect a penny a week from Kensington households.

Three times in the last war the hospital was bombed, but a crisis of a different nature occurred in 1957 when a proposal was entertained to change its general nature to that of a maternity unit of St Mary's Paddington; this was keenly contested by local residents and the matter was raised in the House of Lords. Although the hospital was temporarily reprieved it eventually became a geriatric unit.

St Marylebone Infirmary (since 1922 the St Charles Hospital) began in 1889 in a building which could accommodate 760 patients in five pavilions grouped around a central tower. It was served by an Artesian well and the heating and ventilation system provided a degree of humidity.

Generally speaking, it was safer for a woman to have a child at home since 'childbed fever' was endemic in some of the more crowded hospitals. An appeal in the *Gazette* in 1855 for gifts of 'bundles of swaddling clothes and bed linen' which could be loaned to poor mothers stipulated they would only be given to women who could produce a marriage certificate; any subsequent linen would be lent only if the baby ('if living') was baptised and the mother 'churched'. The death rate of children was very high - in the Dale it was thought that 43 out of every 50 deaths were of children under five years old.

Dentistry was still a primitive skill when Notting Hill was becoming urbanised - herbal and other medicines were quite often taken to relieve toothache. Mr Bellis, a surgeon-dentist of Lonsdale Road, Notting Hill, whose advertisement in the *Gazette* featured a grisly set of enormous false teeth with 'gutta percha' gums, offered the incentive of free extraction of teeth on Tuesdays and Fridays between nine and ten in the morning. The patient could then be fitted out with a set of false teeth which 'required no wires of fastenings'.

John Nodes, the undertaker (his firm is still in business) advertised himself in October 1854 as 'Furnishing Undertaker to the Trade' at 42 Archer Street (Westbourne Grove). He offered a 'Hearse and Pair, Mourning Coach and Pair, with feathers and velvets for horses, elm coffin covered and finished neat, attendance, use of velvet pall and goods for mourners', for £7.10s and the same class 'walking funeral' for £3.5s.

The Canal

In 1783 Parliamentary powers were obtained 'for the making of a Navigable Cut from the Grand Junction Canal in the precinct of Norwood in the County of Middlesex to Paddington', in order to connect the Midlands with the metropolis. At its London end the canal was to cross the northernmost part of Kensington, skirting the Harrow Road and cutting through Westbourne Green to end in a large basin covering much of the area now occupied by Praed Street and Paddington station.

Its half mile through Kensington passed through a small part of the Notting Barns farmland, then known as Smith's Farm. It was opened in June 1801 and on 10 July that year a public inauguration took place when a barge full of dignitaries arrived at Paddington basin 'amid the ringing of bells and the firing of cannon'; a huge crowd gathered to 'hurrah the mighty men' responsible for this new form of water transport in London. For the next twenty or so years the canal enjoyed great popularity, both commercial and as a leisure facility, with passenger boats to Uxbridge plying five times a week and pleasure trips on a barge called the Canal Accommodation Boat. Barges carrying bricks and sand brought supplies to the many building developments along the way, and rubbish was transported on the return journey to burn in the brickfields. Wharves were built along Kensal Road, such as Taft's Wharf, the site of the old Paddington Baths and Wash Houses. Although the Paddington basin lost much of its commercial custom after the opening of the Regent's Canal in 1820 (a canal that linked the canal system with the London docks), the Grand Junction remained a social attraction, and many pictures exist showing excursion steam boats with passengers in mid-Victorian dress enjoying cheap trips during the summer months. Even into the late 19th century rowing boats could be hired from Piner's Boatyard near the Great Western Road, or Sunday School treat parties were taken to Greenford by means of Brook's barges.

The farmlands of Notting Hill were crossed by two brooks, tributaries of the boundary stream, Counter's Creek. One rose near the Plough Inn at Kensal Green, the other near Portobello Farm, running at the foot of St John's Hill where fields with names such as the Meads and Marshes indicated the wet nature of

137. The opening of the Paddington Canal on 10 July 1801.

138. *The Canal in 1804.*

139. *The Grand Junction Canal in North Kensington in recent years.*

the land. These streams were easily crossed by foot-bridge but the canal was a larger obstacle and the need to bridge it became an important factor in property development, especially after the construction of the railway in 1837 when Kensal Town became isolated from the rest of north Kensington, with only one public bridge at first giving access.

It was originally intended that Golborne Road would cross Kensal Road and the Canal to meet Harrow Road, but the Paddington Canal Company placed the footbridge at a place where no thoroughfare existed, and charged a halfpenny toll to use it, gaining it the nickname of the 'Halfpenny Steps'. This was later replaced by the Wedlake Street bridge.

In its early days it was intended that the Canal should also provide water supplies to the districts through which it passed and the Grand Junction Water Works originally drew its supply via the canal from the rivers Brent and Colne. When this proved unsatisfactory the Company returned to the Thames with works at Kew and, as we have seen, at Campden Hill.

Claims to Fame

The southern slopes of Campden Hill around Melbury Road are rich in Pre-Raphaelite and other artists who made their homes there and have been claimed by Kensington as its own, but blue plaques commemorating distinguished residents become sparse as one goes northwards in the borough. However, the northern area has had its full share of those who have contributed to national life.

Much neglected is the literary champion of Notting Hill, Gilbert Keith Chesterton (1874-1936), who lived very briefly in the house of his birth, 32 Sheffield Terrace, but recalled in his autobiography that it was while wandering about the streets of North Kensington that 'something irrationally arrested and pleased my eye about the look of one small block of little lighted shops and I amused myself with the suggestion that these alone were to be preserved and defended like a hamlet in a desert and the first fantastic notion of a tale called *The Napoleon of Notting Hill* rushed over my mind.' That tale, published in 1904, was only a fragment of his literary career and he lived in many other parts of the area during his lifetime, although the family name and the estate agents that bear it have had close links with Kensington and Notting Hill for over 170 years. G.K's sister-in-law, Mrs Cecil Chesterton, made her contribution to Notting Hill by her humane interest in the plight of derelict and impoverished women; she took over an old lodging house in Kensal Road in 1929 which developed into the Cecil Houses hostel movement.

Chesterton found that Kensington, with its historic street names, reminded him of Macaulay's *Essays* and, of course, Macaulay himself spent the last years of his life at Holly Lodge on Campden Hill. In this street there have been numerous famous residents. John Galsworthy (1867-1933), the novelist, came to live in South House, Campden Hill Road, from 1897 to 1903, moving to 16a Aubrey Walk for two years and then on to 14 Addison Road from 1905-13; he also allowed one of his Forsytes to take up residence in the Ladbroke area.

Nearby, at South Lodge (No. 80) lived the writer, Violet Hunt, who could well have been a *Saga* character. The daughter of the Victorian landscape artist, Alfred William Hunt, the flamboyant and eccentric Violet, a hippy before the time, had moved a short distance from her father's house at Tor Villas (which had also once housed Edward Lear) - the house was destroyed by a bomb during the war. At South Lodge she and her 'paying guest', Ford Madox Ford (1873-1939), editor of the distinguished journal *The English Review,* attracted the literary lions of their day to their salon - Henry James, Ezra Pound (who was living in Church Walk), Joseph Conrad, Arnold Bennett, H.G. Wells and many others.

The 'South' of South Lodge is not directional but commemorative of the residence of Sir James South,

140. G.K. Chesterton

141. John Galsworthy

142. *William Mulready*

Callcott specialised in paintings of sea coasts and ships, such as the *Entrance to the Pool of London*. His wife, Maria, achieved fame in her own right as the author of children's books, including *Little Arthur's History of England*. Callcott's home was a centre of artistic life for many years. His brother, John, was a musician and the many visitors included Dr William Crotch (1775-1847), the musician and first principal of the Royal Academy of Music, who was renting a house nearby. Poor Dr Crotch's career was shattered when he was caught kissing a girl student and had to resign.

George Morland (1763-1804), a prolific painter, went to an early grave after a lifetime of excessive drinking. His subjects were usually inns, stables and rural life. He died near the Plough Inn at Kensal Green.

A Royal Academician, J.S. Cooper, whose work also featured landscape and cattle, lived at 42 Chepstow Villas for 34 years of his long life, painting almost to the time of his death at the age of 99 in 1902. Another late Victorian artist, James Pryde, who gained fame in the 1890s for his posters in collaboration with Sir William Nicholson, lived at Lansdowne House until his death in 1941. This was also the address of the artist, Glyn Philpot (1884-1937), for a number of years, while the writer and artist, Percy Wyndham Lewis (1882-1957), lived until his death at 29 Notting Hill Studios.

Another poster artist of great popularity, John Hassall, whose work was part of the London scene for decades, lived in Kensington Park Road, in a house later occupied by his equally talented daughter, the wood engraver, Joan Hassall, and his son, the poet and lyricist, Christopher.

Half way up Campden Street there is a tall, pinnacled building that was known as 'The Studio'. This was the Byam Shaw School of Drawing and Painting, founded by John Byam Shaw and Rex Vicat Cole in 1910, to combine the best of traditional disciplines with modern ideas. The building was constructed with long slits in its facades to allow the movement of canvases too large to pass through its doors. (The school moved to Holloway in the 1980s.)

The society portrait painter, Philip de Laszlo, had his studio for a number of years in West House, on the corner of Campden Hill Road and Peel Street, a Norman Shaw house originally designed for the American painter, George Henry Boughton (1837-1905), while at Peel Cottage nearby, William Russell Flint was creating his pictures of flamenco gipsies.

Sir Hugh Casson has had several addresses in Notting Hill, including Elgin Crescent, but his interest in the whole area has been constant since his participation in the foundation of the Kensington Society. In the 1950s, in collaboration with Neville Conder, he designed the adaptation of the ruins of

the astronomer, who bought this 18th-century mansion which had once been the family home of the Phillimores, in 1827. South built an observatory in the garden and even though he received advice from Isambard Kingdom Brunel he was dissatisfied with the construction of the dome and followed this up with a lawsuit against the maker of his telescope. When he lost the case he vented his anger by breaking up the instrument and selling it for scrap at a much-publicised auction in his garden. South's irascibility is further demonstrated by his refusal to allow a road to pass near his house for fear the vibration from traffic should interfere with his astronomical observations: Campden Hill Road was only opened to traffic at its southern end after South's death.

Although Jonathan (Dean) Swift (1667-1745) is believed to have lodged in the Gravel Pits area in 1712, probably the earliest residents to give Notting Hill Gate an association with the arts were the Royal Academicians, William Mulready (1786-1863) and Augustus Wall Callcott (1779-1844). They lived within a stone's throw of each other, Callcott in a terrace on the site of the present Essex Church, in a house where he had been born and where he died, and Mulready, the son of an Irish leather worker, between the Mall and Church Street; on his marriage, at the age of nineteen, he moved to Linden Grove.

Mulready is popularly remembered for his design for a postal envelope for Sir Rowland Hill; one of his most famous paintings is *Choosing the Wedding Gown*.

Holland House into the Youth Hostel, and he is now the President of the Friends of Holland Park.

Victorian artist, Sir Frank Dicksee, had a studio at 80 Peel Street while not so far from him at the same time, E.A. Abbey RA was living at 54 Bedford Gardens, the same street where the artist and cartoonist, Ronald Searle, had a studio in the 1950s. William Cleverley Alexander, who bought Aubrey House in the 1870s, was a great collector and patron of the arts. It was his daughter, Cecily, who was the model for Whistler's *Harmony in Grey and Green*. Although brought up as members of the Society of Friends, Alexander and his wife joined the Church of England but continued in the simple Quaker way of life. Their three daughters, Cecily, Rachel and Jean, spent their lives at Aubrey House and after their father's death in 1916 presented most of his paintings and *objects d'art* to the Victoria & Albert Museum, converting the two wings of the house into flats. Miss Rachel, a small, unobtrusive woman in the plainest of dress, was a tireless worker for social and housing voluntary bodies in North Kensington. She died in 1964. Her friend, Mary (Baroness) Stocks, the academic and well-known broadcaster, lived for many years at Aubrey Lodge until her death in 1975.

One of the very few old houses still remaining in Kensington Church Street is No. 128, which was the home for many years of the composer, Muzio Clementi (1752-1832). In more recent times, the spirit behind many successful Victorian and Edwardian theatrical productions, Charles Hayden Coffin (1862-1922), lived in Bedford Gardens for nearly thirty years until his death, while the popular music-hall star, Albert Chevalier (1861-1923), was born at 17 (then 21) St Ann's Villas. Eugene Sandow (1867-1925), the body builder, lived at 16 Holland Park Avenue from 1907 to 1925. The lugubrious comedian, Robertson Hare (1891-1979), lived in Holland Park Avenue in the 1930s, though he moved south to Warwick Gardens in his later years when his unmistakeable features were often seen in the local supermarkets or bus queues delighting his fans in *All Gas and Gaiters*.

Notting Hill's several connections with *Punch* include the residence for a time at 62 Holland Park Avenue of John Leech, whose drawings were such a popular feature in the journal between 1841-64, while another contributor, Phil May, lived at 11 Campden Hill Square in 1899. Hablot Knight Browne (1815-82), better known as the artist-illustrator 'Phiz' for Charles Dickens's books, lived at 99 Ladbroke Grove from 1872-80.

The novelist, Katherine Mansfield, and the man she eventually married, John Middleton Murry, had homes in various parts of west London and among them was 95 Elgin Crescent. The writer, Monica Dickens (1915-93), who used her true life experiences

143. *Katherine Mansfield.*

144. *John Leech.*

in journalism, nursing and other occupations as the basis for her fiction, was a life-long resident of the area (her father was the veteran alderman, Henry Dickens) until her death in 1993.

Wilson Carlile, the founder of the Church Army, lived at 34 Sheffield Terrace when he was working as a curate at St Mary Abbots in 1880. His evangelical services shocked some of the staid congregation but drew large crowds to halls and open air meetings. There is no record of the impression he might have made on Evelyn Underhill, the Christian philosopher (1875-1941), who was only a child at the time, although she lived later at 50 Campden Hill Square from 1907 until shortly before her death. A prolific author on the subject of Zen Buddhism as well as being a Circuit Judge, Travers Christmas Humphreys, was born at 7 Royal Crescent in 1901 and lived in the area for many years. His interest led to his founding of the Buddhist Society in Britain, whose journal was printed for many years by the publishers of the *Kensington News*, James Wakeham in Church Street. A writer who might be regarded as the father of the Green movement, the naturalist, William Hudson, lived at 40 St Luke's Road in his last years, and a plaque was erected there by his admirers.

Louis Kossuth (1802-94), the ardent Hungarian nationalist, imprisoned for his liberal views, came to England in 1851 to try to organise a mass uprising of patriots, and stayed at 39 Chepstow Villas. Guglielmo Marconi (1874-1937), the pioneer of wireless communication, came to London and 71 Hereford Road in 1896. His neighbour at 7 Kensington Park Gardens was the scientist, Sir William Crookes (1832-1919), whose innumerable achievements included the discovery of the element Thalium in 1861. He lived at this address from 1880 until his death.

Residents of Notting Hill who achieved their fame in far-away places include Field Marshal Sir John Burgoyne (1782-1871), who served under Wellington in the Peninsular War; he died at 5 Pembridge Square. John Stuart (1815-66), the first explorer to cross Australia and after whom Mount Stuart is named, lived at 9 Campden Hill Square.

Notting Hill's connection with politicians was unusually slender until Roy (now Lord) Jenkins came to live at 33 Ladbroke Square in 1959; his wife, Dame Jennifer, devoted much of her time working with the North Kensington Amenity Trust. Lloyd George lived

145. George Morland, from a drawing by Thomas Rowlandson

at 2 Addison Road from 1928 until 1938. Campden Hill Square enjoyed some notoriety when a house there, owned by a Mrs Brackenbury, became known as 'Mouse Castle', a derisive nickname for a centre for suffragettes. It was used as a refuge for women temporarily released from prison and the forced feeding they endured under Asquith's 'Cat and Mouse' policy. Mrs Brackenbury's daughter, Georgina, caused consternation when she managed to get herself smuggled into the House of Lords in a furniture van. 'Painted Corner', a shop on the corner of Edge Street, decked out in the colours of the Women's Social and Political Union, green, purple and white, became the local suffragette headquarters.

Kensal Green Cemetery

By the early decades of the 19th century the population of London had increased so rapidly that its old churchyards could no longer cope with the interment of the dead. Charles Dickens vividly described the macabre sights and noxious smells of overcrowded graveyards.

It was to alleviate this situation that in the 1830s and 1840s Parliament authorised the establishment of cemetery companies, the first of these being the General Cemetery Company, who formed Kensal Green Cemetery in the fields north of the Grand Junction Canal on the highest point of Kensington, 150 feet above sea level.

Some ten years earlier, a London barrister, George Frederick Carden, inspired by the Père-Lachaise cemetery in Paris, began looking around the outskirts of London for a site where a similar burial ground could be created. Designs were produced by several leading architects, and by the 1830s Carden had formed a provisional committee to deal with the

project. Their architect, Francis Goodwin, envisaged a cemetery with temples, mausolea, cloisters and catacombs, 'a very magnificent display of architecture in 42 acres of garden'. Andrew Spottiswoode MP, a friend of Carden's, presented a petition to Parliament 'praying for the removal of the metropolitan graveyards to places where they would be less prejudicial to the health of the inhabitants', and one of the members of the committee, Sir John Dean Paul, purchased the 54 acres of woodland and pasture at Kensal Green for £9,500. A cholera epidemic in 1831 fired public support for the concept of such cemeteries - it was widely believed then that the disease was carried by the miasma of foul air, and the removal of burial grounds out of the metropolis was therefore advisable.

There was dispute between the committee and Carden as to the style of their cemetery. Should it be Grecian, as Paul wanted, or Gothic, as Carden preferred? An architectural competition resulted in H.E. Kendall winning with his romantic vision of towers and pinnacles of Arthurian splendour, with a watergate entrance from the Grand Junction Canal - a practical touch at a time when transport to Kensal Green was difficult. But Kendall's plan did not come to fruition, for the Classicists won in the end and

146. Kensal Green Cemetery c1845.

147. *Kensal Green Cemetery c1845.*

Carden was dismissed. John Griffith (who had been one of the judges) was awarded the job of designing the Church of England chapel in the Doric style.

The entrance gate and catacombs were also by Griffith. The latter, a series of brick vaults built in a curve, were furnished with stone coffin racks and cast-iron protective grilles. To here, the coffins, often elaborately covered with velvet, could be lowered on a hydraulic lift at the end of the committal service, a very novel facility then.

The Cemetery, dedicated to All Souls, was consecrated on 24 January 1833 and the first interment took place a week later. Thousands of trees were planted over the grounds and even as late as 1924 Florence Gladstone in *Notting Hill in Bygone Days* was able to say 'the view from the terrace in front of the cemetery church is still beautiful'.

Miss Gladstone also added that although many disapproved of the waste involved in the huge mausolea and ranks of tombstones, they provided a unique record of Victorian taste. Among the most distinguished dead there is the Duke of Sussex, brother of George IV, who had been so shocked by the unseemly confusion at the funeral of his brother, William IV, at Windsor, that he swore he would never be buried there. His sister, Sofia, lies in a grave nearby, as does his nephew, the second Duke of Cambridge

A magnificent monument marks the graves of the Ducrow family (Andrew Ducrow was a circus rider and theatrical impresario); it is a vaguely Chinese-looking temple guarded by benevolent stone lions. Facets of Victorian life are represented - Blondin, the acrobat; Isambard Kingdom Brunel and his father, Marc Brunel, the civil engineers; architect Decimus Burton; the writers William Makepeace Thackeray, Harrison Ainsworth, Wilkie Collins and Anthony Trollope; the poet, Thomas Hood; the essayist, Leigh Hunt; John Leech, the illustrator; Henry Mayhew, author of the classic social history, *London Labour and the London Poor*; John Loudon, the landscape gardener, and Thomas Wakley, social reformer and editor of *The Lancet* magazine.

Adjoining is the Roman Catholic cemetery of St Mary's, which is actually outside the borough boundary. This opened in 1858 and provided a last resting place for thousands of immigrant Irish who came to London in search of work during the Great Famine. Among more recent interments there have been those of Gilbert Harding, the TV personality, and the conductor, Sir John Barbirolli, in 1970.

The Phoenix of Queensway

William Whiteley came to London practically penniless. He took a little shop in Westbourne Grove ('Bankrupt Avenue' they called it then) and built it into London's first mighty emporium, the 'Universal Provider', which delighted the new carriage trade moving into the new estates of Pembridge and Ladbroke in Notting Hill, but angered local traders so much that they staged riots and even burned the effigy of the 'most hated man in London'.

Whiteley was born in Agbrigg near Leeds in September 1831. He left school at the age of fourteen and went to work on his uncle's farm, but after a couple of years persuaded his parents to apprentice him to a draper in Wakefield. In 1851 the Whiteleys, in common with thousands of other families, made the adventurous journey to London to see the Great Exhibition, and Wakefield no longer seemed impressive to young William, who returned north but only long enough to save £10 and come back to take a job with a draper's in the City of London.

As he learned, he saved, and when he had £700 in the bank he decided to risk everything and open his own business in a street of dilapidated shops: 'William Whiteley - Ribbons and Fancy Goods'. When his first customer entered she took an immediate liking to the young man and asked if she could offer up a prayer for his future success; she did, and they remained friends until his death. It was an effective prayer, for in two years staff and shops had doubled, and by 1872 he had bought up premises all along the street. The scope of the business increased to include an estate agency, dry cleaning and other services. He shocked the local magistrates by applying for a wine licence so that husbands could enjoy a drink while their wives toured the store. But the fat was really in the fire, so to speak, when he opened a butcher's department. The local butchers demonstrated outside armed with marrow bones and cleavers.

148. The Whiteley's store in its heyday

149. One of the numerous fires at the Whiteley store - this one portrayed by the Illustrated London News *in 1887.*

Whiteley worked hard himself and did not spare his staff. Their hours were 7am to 11pm and as they lived above the premises there was every reason for them to be punctual. In 1867, with shops stretching along both sides of Westbourne Grove and in Queensway, Whiteley married Sarah Hill, but his commercial success was not joined with marital happiness, and it was soon rumoured that he had a mistress.

He made numerous enemies among the local traders - in 1876 an effigy of him was burnt on Guy Fawkes' Night, and a few years later there was a disastrous fire when both sides of his emporium were gutted at a loss of £42,000, fortunately covered by insurance. But six weeks later a new block of his shops was also alight. The origins of both fires remained a mystery.

Three more fires occurred. In April 1884 a row of five shops was destroyed and a few months later another large blaze had to be fought. And then, in 1887, while Whiteley was abroad, thousands of people came from all over London to see a new blaze and hawkers did a roaring trade selling food to the sightseers, while 34 of London's 45 steam fire engines pumped water on to the buildings.

Despite these setbacks Whiteley always recovered, holding mammoth salvage sales which attracted large numbers. By the turn of the century he was employing 6,000 people and had a turnover of £1 million.

His violent death matched his spectacular career. On 24 January 1907 he was shot outside his office by an assailant who had gained entry by saying he had come from Whiteley's solicitor. The two were alone in Whiteley's office for a time and when they came out the store owner asked an assistant to find a policeman. The visitor then pulled out a gun and shot Whiteley twice, killing him instantly, and then shot himself in the head.

He recovered and stood trial in the name of Horace George Rayner, but he claimed to be an illegitimate son of Whiteley. He was sentenced to death but later reprieved to serve life imprisonment.

The store that Whiteley founded had been formed into a public company in 1899 and in 1911, when the old leases fell in, the Board decided to move the entire store to Queensway. The central dome of the new building was on the site of the old Paddington Baths, and its grand staircase is still treasured. Whiteley's remained in the control of his descendants until it was bought by Selfridge's in 1927. The building was closed in 1981 but reopened eight years later as a complex of shops, restaurants and cinemas.

150. *All Saints Road c1900. Eggs are 8d a dozen and 'Country milk' is sold direct from the farm by Thomas's Dairy.*

Rachman and Riots

CLEARING THE SLUMS

Until the end of the Second World War the usual description of the neighbourhood north of Holland Park Avenue up as far as the Harrow Road was 'North Kensington'. 'Notting Hill' was yet to be born as a journalistic shorthand for the area and it was in the 'North Kensington' constituency that the Labour candidate, Corporal George Rogers, defeated the Conservative, Captain J.A.L. Duncan, in the first post-war General Election.

A few months later, in September 1946, a column of homeless families from the East End assembled at Kensington High Street station and marched up Campden Hill to invade the blocks of luxury flats which had been requisitioned during the war to house refugees from Malta and Gibraltar and were now standing empty. About 300 people camped out in Duchess of Bedford House while others occupied Moray Lodge and other empty houses in Upper Phillimore and Phillimore Gardens. Their final eviction needed a High Court injunction.

In the early 1950s large demolition schemes began in all parts of North Kensington. 'Blitz on 3,000 slum houses' said a *Kensington News* headline in 1955, but it conceded that there was still the problem of finding new homes for the displaced families. No one could argue that slum clearance was not necessary, nor long overdue, but those who moved away from the

squalid streets to more hygienic surroundings did not always appreciate their 'good fortune', so that even today Bangor Street is not recalled as an over-crowded slum but as a homely, friendly place, where there was true neighbourliness, with only petty crime and an old rag fair on Sundays.

As the bulldozers knocked down the low-rise streets, West Indians, many working for London Transport, were moving into the remaining terraces. In 1956, a young photographer, Roger Mayne, made a pictorial study of the triangle between Wood Lane and the Harrow Road, where Teddy Boys vied with uncertain West Indian youths in broad-brimmed fedoras, but the sound of steel bands and the sight of yams on the market stalls were still as yet unknown.

The immigrants suffered particularly in the housing shortage, and their obvious presence, both physical and cultural, in an overcrowded area served as an irritant to those whites already competing for accommodation and jobs. In 1959, Sir Oswald Mosley, whose Union Party had been active in the area, stood for Parliament. He was unsuccessful, but the fact that he chose to stand was significant. In May that year, the name of Perc Rachman, a Polish refugee and smalltime landlord, came first into public notice.

The 1957 Rent Act had brought to an end many of the old rent restrictions which had prevailed for over forty years. As a result unfurnished accommodation

151. *Demonstrators against the 1957 Rent Act canvassing in Notting Hill.*

152. *A soap-box speaker addresses a street-corner meeting in Portobello Road against the 1957 Rent Act.*

became rare, and Rent Tribunals were set up to control exorbitant charges for furnished accommodation which, with the provision of a few sticks of furniture, could escape most regulations.

AN INFAMOUS LANDLORD

It was an unusually interesting day at the West London Rent Tribunal on 29 May 1959, where proceedings were usually concerned with the quality of plumbing, the furniture or the curtains. This time the tenants appearing there, who had described their rooms as scruffy, dirty and unfit for human habitation, also said that they and others had been threatened by strong-arm men if they made their complaints public. These thugs included Michael de Freitas, later known in the United States as 'Michael X', who was eventually executed there for murder. The properties under scrutiny were in Powis Square, and were said to be owned by a Mr Perc Rachman. This was the first time that London people, other than those personally involved, had heard the name which was to be featured in many headlines and which has become part of the English language.

Immigrant families were the most vulnerable to Rachman's methods - and he was not the only landlord employing them. Blackmail and bullying attacks were used to evict people from their low-rent apartments so that they could be relet at much higher rents, some to prostitutes on a daily basis. Illegal gaming parties went on for days on end, and drunkenness and brawling were all part of the landlords' armoury to harass and force out unfortunate tenants.

This state of affairs was public knowledge in the locality for four years before the John Profumo case in 1963 brought the matter into the national press. Rachman, who had an association with Mandy Rice Davies, one of the key personalities in the Profumo

affair, was exposed by Ben Parkin, MP for Paddington, in the House of Commons, where he was protected by privilege. Things were harder for newspapers, who were wary of libel laws and writs from Rachman.

RACE RIOTS

What was divulged about the state of things in Notting Hill (as the area was now called by journalists) only served to confirm the area's poor reputation, which had been formed in the Race Riots of 1958. In the riots gangs of white youths roamed the streets off Ladbroke Grove and All Saints Road attacking black people and their property, and black youths retaliated. Compared with subsequent riots in more recent years and in different areas of the country, they were small affairs, but they assumed national importance because of their novelty and because of their relevance to many communities.

The Mayor of Kensington set up a race relations committee and the Methodist church delegated three young ministers to build up multi-racial congregations. It was this group ministry which formed the Notting Hill Social Council, a forum of clergy, community and social workers. Bruce Kendrick, a Presbyterian minister, who formed Shelter, the national campaign for the homeless, set up the Notting Hill Housing Trust in 1963 which has done much good work in the area by modernising and managing scores of low-rent apartments.

153. This drawing of the ruins of Holland House, before its partial demolition after war damage, was made in the early 1950s by the artist, David Thomas, for a series in the Kensington News.

The Kensington Society

In March 1953 a group of people who shared a common concern about the amenities and the past of Kensington met in a house in Kensington Square. They included Sir Hugh Casson, Oliver Messel, Lord Gorell, Ashley Dukes, Professor Arnold Toynbee, Sir William Russell Flint, Mr. C. Boxall (the Kensington Reference Librarian and an authority on local history), Dr Stephen Pasmore (a keen amateur historian), and the woman in whose house they met, Mrs Gay Christiansen. Thus the Kensington Society came into existence and, as it happened, not a moment too soon, for within months an emergency meeting had to be called to discuss the future of Holland House.

Rachel Ferguson, a keen supporter of the Society, had already written in her book *Royal Borough* (1950): 'Although its graceful shell remains it is largely gutted...the two entrance lodges blasted. What will the Ilchesters do? Is this historic mansion to go the beastly modern way and be patched up by some soulless community purpose or sold and razed for high-class flats? Could and would any government - let alone the present one - allot the compensation for careful repair? Will we Kensingtonians be invited to band together to save the place?'

When the Society was formed, demolition had already begun and was due to be completed by May 1954. It was decided then that every effort should be made to save at least the east wing, which was less badly damaged. Deputations were organised, letters appeared in *The Times* and public meetings were arranged. Finally, an agreement was reached to incorporate the remains of the house in the King George VI Memorial Youth Hostel, and the parkland was opened to the public - surely the Society's greatest achievement.

During its forty years the Society has naturally had to concentrate on the 'great and good' areas of central and southern Kensington, but the more northerly parts have not been forgotten, particularly the artists' colony around the old centre of Campden Hill. It also successfully opposed a scheme to build two 23-storey blocks on the crest of the hill. In more recent years it has also acted as a liaison and support body for numerous neighbourhood societies such as the Norland Conservation Society, Campden Street Preservation Society, the Ladbroke Association, the Pembridge Association and others. Mrs Christiansen, who was instrumental in its founding, is still serving as its Honorary Secretary, and much of its success has been due to her dogged persistence.

The Portobello Attraction

A narrow, rather dismal thoroughfare, lined on either side with terraces of small and sometimes shabby shops, the pavements fringed with street traders' stalls, has become a tourist attraction to rival Westminster Abbey and the Tower of London. Portobello Road market has no equal anywhere in the world.

Sixty years ago, or even less, it was still little more than any other street market, though elevated on Saturdays by the presence of antique or junk stalls, but by the end of the last war the increasingly cosmopolitan character of Notting Hill and the growing interest in things antiquarian, raised its status. It changed from a neighbourhood market to an international attraction.

This would have surprised Shoggy Warren, who in 1920 obliged the local housewives with buckets of coal from his coal-cum-junk shop on the corner of 'the Lane', as the locals call it, and Bolton Road (which disappeared with the building of Portobello Court in the 1960s). Shoggy was recalled by Mr R.L. Shepherd, who had spent all his boyhood in North Kensington. Son of the local Pearly King and Queen, Shepherd had retired to Wantage when he wrote his recollections for the *Kensington News* in the 1970s. He remembered the days 'when you could take a sack or bucket to Shoggy Warren, who would fill it with seven pounds of coal for threepence...but as coal could be bought for two shillings a hundredweight

154. The Notting Barns and the Portobello Farms. Map drawn by the Author.

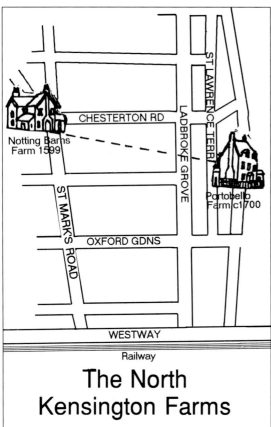

The North Kensington Farms

155. The Portobello Estate. Map drawn by the Author.

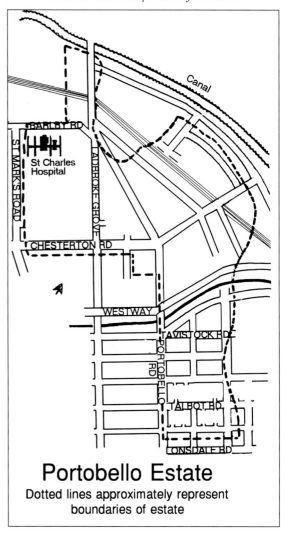

Portobello Estate
Dotted lines approximately represent boundaries of estate

156. Portobello Farmhouse. From a sepia drawing by W.E. Wellings.

[112 pounds] this concession to the hard up brought in good profits'. It is easy to understand why the three houses next to the shop also belonged to the Warrens! The houses were painted red, white and blue for the Coronation of George V, much to the amusement of the neighbours. The picture painted by Shepherd was as colourful as a Hogarth print, depicting life that was rough, raucous and often squalid and impoverished. A booklet produced in 1882 by an anonymous 'Old Inhabitant' records that until the middle of the 19th century Portobello Road was one of the most rural and pleasant walks in London, and Thomas Faulkner in his *History of the Antiquities of Kensington* (1820) noted that nothing could be heard there in the tranquil silence 'but the notes of the lark, the linnet and the nightingale'.

A wide green lane when it left Notting Hill Gate, the byway narrowed as it went northwards. To the east were the fields known as the barley shots (a shot being a small parcel of land) and half a mile or so onwards the lane became a footpath after passing Portobello Farm. The farm had been purchased by Charles Henry Talbot of the Inner Temple in 1755 and the 170 acres were let out to a farmer called Adams for £170 a year. It took its name, as did the road eventually, from Admiral Vernon's capture of Puerto Bello in the Gulf of Mexico from the Spaniards in 1739.

Two other farms existed in this area north of Holland Park Avenue: Norlands, last farmed by Joseph Higgins in 1847, when it was bought up, together with Norlands House, for the building of streets around St James's Gardens, and Notting Barns on land now covered by the Lancaster West Estate.

The freehold of the Portobello farm area was still owned by the Talbot family in the 1850s when land values had risen considerably. In 1852, after some land had been sold to the Great Western Railway and the gas company for £1,000 per acre, more was bought by the ill-fated Dr Walker. The farm house was also offered for sale but it was not until 1864 that it was bought by the Little Sisters of the Poor, from Brittany, who used it to establish their St Joseph's Home for the Aged, now the site of council housing. Another convent, founded by Dr (later Cardinal) Henry Manning, already existed on the west side of Portobello Road, belonging to the Franciscan Order of Poor Clares, and later sold to a Dominican Order. This convent incorporated the St Elizabeth Home for Children and the extensive grounds, covering about two acres, included a burial ground for nuns who died there - they were later reinterred in St Mary's Roman Catholic Cemetery at Kensal Green. The buildings are now used by a Spanish college.

The Metropolitan Railway bridge crosses Portobello Road at the point where the old lane ran through

157. *Another market in the Notting Hill area was the Rag Fair held on Sunday mornings in Bangor Street.*

158. *A 1905 view of an early Marks and Spencer's at 233 Portobello Road. It was one of their 'Penny Bazaars', with the goods out on stands.*

159. Carter's fish shop at 150 Portobello Road c1911.

a marshy patch of rushes and watercress, once popular with hunters shooting snipe. Just north of Portobello Farm the lane divided in two, the path to the right leading across meadowland to Kensal Road, crossing the GWR line by a level crossing, the other path, which eventually provided the route for the road to Kensal Green, crossed the railway and the canal by a footbridge.

Although the area to the east was already being developed, the lane itself remained comparatively rural until 1864 apart from a single half-built house, known as 'The Folly'. The Warwick Castle on the

160. *Sale of the Portobello farmland and house in 1854.*

corner of Cornwall Road (now Westbourne Park Road) was the successor of a small inn of the same name. But within less than ten years, houses and shops had gone up on both sides of the road (although until 1919 the stalls hardly extended beyond the railway arches). The houses on the west side had been built as private dwellings but shops were soon built out over their front gardens. On the opposite side they began life as shops, one of the earliest being a draper's owned by William H. Gough, at Nos. 146-150, founded in 1859. There was a timber yard of Messrs Horsman at No. 191, and a corn chandler's on the corner of Elgin Crescent owned by John Green, a Kensington vestryman who had also made a name for himself as the inventor of a musical notation to teach the Ragged School children to sing hymns. Another trader, Charlton Frye, represented Kensington in Parliament and on the LCC.

In its earlier days Portobello Market functioned only on weekdays until the stallholders won over the Vestry to allow trading six days a week. In 1927 an LCC Act established this and other street markets in London on an official basis with licensed stalls and Market Inspectors to ensure compliance with rules

161. *Portobello Road at the turn of the century.*

162. *W. Edwards' fruit stall in the Portobello Road in the 1920s. Bananas are 2d each and 'Sound tomatoes' are at 4d a half pound.*

163. A Portobello pavement furniture 'showroom' in the 1960s.

164. A stall owner takes a rest..

over areas used for display and health and safety regulations.

Nowadays, the antique market overshadows the old provision stalls, but the coster market tradition is still strong there, and is particularly noticeable on occasions when one of the long-standing coster families dies. A long procession of cars follows the hearse up a respectfully silent street, and there are intimate floral tributes in the shape of favourite chairs, a pipe, or some other object connected with the deceased.

165. The Dominican convent at 317a Portobello Road, now a college.

All Change

The appearance of Notting Hill Gate today is a result of a comprehensive redevelopment at the end of the 1950s. The improvement and widening of the road here was a perennial topic of Kensington Vestry and its successor, the Kensington Borough Council, for over a century. It was not until 1937 that the LCC obtained powers to widen the street and £1 million was approved to cover the cost. However, the outbreak of war postponed the work and it was not until 1957 that the final scheme materialised, involving a co-operative effort between the LCC, London Transport and the property developer, Jack Cotton. The result, according to Simon Jenkins in his *Landlords to London*, was 'a wider road and two blankly characterless blocks looming over what had previously been an exciting, diverse London high street'.

Actually, the first two 'characterless blocks' were joined by others, and changed the whole frontage stretching from the hideous grey fortress of the Czech Embassy on the corner of the Mall to the Coronet Theatre. The only terrace to keep its original form was that between Linden Gardens and Pembridge Gardens, where a few older facades survived. During the building of these new blocks, which lasted for three years, the two Underground stations were reconstructed with a combined concourse (previously, those changing from the Circle to the Central line had to cross the road).

The section of redevelopment which extended down the west side of Church Street to Kensington Place swept away not only some attractive but tumble-down shops, but the surgery of Mr Ollerhead, a well-known veterinary surgeon whose premises had facilities for treating horses. Mr Ollerhead continued to treat smaller animals until his retirement at a surgery beneath Mall Chambers, an interesting block of flats built as 'improved dwellings intended for a class somewhat above ordinary mechanics and labourers', although the *Building News* at the time of their construction in 1871 considered the block had 'rather the look of a warehouse'. Its residents included a surgeon, a stockbroker's clerk and a librarian, as well as plumbers, porters and painters, so it was already climbing towards its present status as a desirable residence.

Rabbit Row, the turning off the Mall at its junction with Church Street, originally housed a block of stables and stalls for nine coaches for Sir Samuel Morton Peto, the wealthy builder and MP, who lived in grandeur in Kensington Palace Gardens. Their site was converted into a meeting hall, which later became a theatre club, and is now occupied by Broadwalk Court, built in 1964.

166. Notting Hill Gate 1947.

167. *Notting Hill Gate 1957, before rebuilding, looking east.*

168. *Demolition at Notting Hill Gate.*

169. *Demolition in the 1950s at the corner of Pembridge Road.*

170. *Older properties at Notting Hill Gate in c1970, which survived the transformation.*

171. The construction of Westway across Ladbroke Grove in the 1960s.

WESTWAY INTRUDER

Another wholesale change, this time to the north of Notting Hill Gate, took place about fifteen years later. Built intrusively on concrete stilts above the down-at-heel neighbourhood of North Kensington came The Road.

Between the end of the First World War and the early 1940s, Westway, an enlarged A40 Oxford Road, was constructed piecemeal, each new section exacerbating bottlenecks at White City and Shepherds Bush. Its extension to Marylebone was long overdue when the decision was taken in the late 1950s to build it as an overhead motorway through the tattered remains of 'Notting Hill'.

'You cannot but have sympathy for these people', said Michael Heseltine, Parliamentary Secretary to the Ministry of Transport at the opening of Westway in 1970, when he was barracked by protesters who had endured the horrors of its four-year construction. Those who were displaced by the road's route may have wept and left, but those left behind on its verges, in places such as Acklam Road, had to go on living in its shadow. 'Get us out of Hell!' was demanded on their banners. It was hardly an overstatement.

Below the motorway, slum clearance and redevelopment, part of a £15 million scheme to transform the Lancaster West area and Kensal New Town, proceeded. This produced Sir William Holford's 6 acre estate with Adair and Hazlewood Towers. To those still living in expensive multi-occupied sleazy homes these were indeed pie in the sky.

The area was ripe for picking and the pickers included not only the great, the good and the charitable, but the politically opportunist. The Community Workshop, the Free School, the Notting Hill People's Association, the Notting Hill Law Centre, the Housing Action Centre etc., were all worthy enterprises, but among those in charge of the borough of Kensington there were fears of left-wing activists. In particular there was Eddie Adams, a well-known member of the local Communist Party and a frequent contender for Golborne ward in elections: the flamboyant Tory Mayor, Sir Malby Crofton, found himself sitting on the same Management Committee of the Notting Hill Amenity Trust as Adams in 1971.

A lack of open space also bedevilled the area. A century earlier, clergy and charity workers had pressed for parks but the response was poor. Avondale Park and the tiny Emslie Horniman Pleasance and the Memorial Park in the north west, a mere twenty acres altogether, were all that materialised. The Kensington and Chelsea Play Association, formed in 1969, set up centres in Acklam Road, Emslie Horniman Pleasance, Powis Square and Lancaster West in a campaign headed by Pat Smythe, who had already worked for ten years at the Notting Hill Adventure Playground.

Between the wars the Harrow and Rugby Clubs had been set up by the public schools of those names, to provide recreation for local young people and later, Jack Banbury, a police officer at Notting Hill Police Station, and his wife, had founded the Dale Club for boys and girls. But these were organised centres with fixed programmes, which still left hundreds of youngsters roaming the streets.

It was in this connection that use was made of the space beneath Westway. The area where the road crossed Notting Hill was already one of dereliction, fly-tipping, vagrants and travellers. In 1969 the Motorway Development Trust (originally a Playspace Group) was set up to make the best use of this Notting Hill eyesore. Response was not encouraging - one questionnaire received only one reply, and sometimes meetings degenerated into political brawls. The local authority was suspicious if not hostile, and personalities and politics clashed. 'It was touch and go as to whether or not it would be a success' said Jennifer Jenkins, who chaired the Trust from 1974 to 1977, for it involved the seemingly impossible task of reconciling a Conservative borough authority with left wing community activists.

Not only were recreational facilities eventually provided, but space was made available for the totters who had been displaced from the various stables and yards and who at one stage drove their carts to Buckingham Palace to convey their plight to the Queen.

There are now a number of business tenancies in this under-road area, which help to fund the recreational schemes and the maintenance of ten acres of open space. It is here that some of the biggest events of the annual Notting Hill Carnival are held, while Portobello Green accommodates the two-day concerts. It is also the venue for celebrations such as the Spanish and Portuguese fiestas, which highlight the presence of another large group of Notting Hill immigrants.

172. *The landscape of North Kensington has changed dramatically since the 1960s with the construction of numerous tower blocks with some hopeful landscaping around them. Trellick Tower, north of the Westway, designed by Erno Goldfinger, is one that has provoked strong feelings, for and against.*

Carnival

It was only two years after the Rachman scandal had claimed national attention and brought Notting Hill notoriety that the Carnival was born, in the most modest manner, at the instigation of a white social worker, Mrs Rhaune Laslett, and a group of West Indian friends. Mrs Laslett, who had been forced to give up full-time work owing to Multiple Sclerosis, set up a voluntary organisation from her home in North Kensington: this was called the Neighbourhood Service, and it helped the homeless, elderly and children in trouble. She thought it a pity that the West Indians had left behind so much of their culture, such as street carnivals, and decided to organise one.

The first celebration took place in 1965, a simple event mainly directed at children. It lasted for eight days and proved a great success. Six years later, in 1971, the Carnival had grown, but was still a local affair organised by a Cultural Development committee consisting mainly of black musicians, such as Selwyn Baptiste, who had introduced steel bands to the Notting Hill Adventure Playground and Russell Henderson, who was playing at the Colherne pub in Earls Court. Others involved were Theo Stephens and Sterling Betancourt, members of the first team of steel band musicians to be sent to this country from the Caribbean. Mrs Laslett donated the costumes from earlier carnivals to help out the tight budget and outsiders taking part were still limited to a few groups of children from other parts of London.

From these small beginnings the Carnival has become an almost international event and, with this growth, there have been severe problems of crowd control. Now concentrated on the late Summer Bank Holiday weekend its size has become in many ways an embarrassment, and there has been unwelcome commercial and media exploitation. The actual event lasts three days, but planning goes on all year.

There have been some exceedingly troublesome carnivals and even tragedies, but it survives as a mainly joyous and successful event in which different cultures meet, for once, on common ground.

173. A spectacular costume at the Carnival.

A Fragile Peace

A twenty-minute walk northwards from Notting Hill Gate will encounter leafy and pretty streets and then, nearby, much slum property, for despite valiant efforts there are grim reminders of the poverty of many of the residents. Also, though there have been substantial improvements in the look of the better properties, the actual thoroughfare of Notting Hill Gate is uglier in its new clothes and less interesting than it was. Away from the desirability of Holland Park, but not too far from the concentration of antique shops and boutiques, there is a contrasting world. At the north-west end of Ladbroke Grove, across the 'Meccano' railway bridge, painted liver-blood red, Sainsbury's reigns against a background of new gasholders and sheds. On the other side of the road, descend the steps to Southern Row, into a land of local authority estates and wary pedestrians. Even at noon on a sunny weekday there are few people about, so that a group of youths on a street corner can seem threatening. The shabby old cottages of Middle, East and West Rows have long since gone, replaced by a motley and undistinguished collection of buildings, and there are dismal wire fences and weedy patches; set against a tower block Emslie Horniman Pleasance seems meanly small, despite its spring blossom; Golborne Road is reached past concrete walls, and the railway bridge is heavily fly-posted and ugly. In the road itself a travel agent, a patisserie and ethnic boutiques rub shoulders with the Golborne Advice Centre; the Golborne Free Church is now 'Peake House', freshly painted white and blue and the home of the evangelical Christian Alliance.

The Caernarvon Castle pub survives in Victorian solidity on the corner of Bevington Road, but from there to the motorway Portobello Road is featureless between the back walls of the council estate and those of the old Dominican Convent, now a college. Only past the bridges does the weekday market become trendily tatty and busy.

It is here that failure to redeem the post-Motorway dereliction is painfully obvious. Prettily named Portobello Green has grass and trees, even some flowers, but the shrubs are downtrodden and litter-strewn; the motorway pillars are scrawled with graffiti and tattered with posters, the brick-paved walkway is unswept. Failed businesses and empty shops threaten a new slide to slumdom.

Those who have tried so hard to achieve improvement in this area may find this description unnecessarily pessimistic, as though the area is beyond redemption. But the reality of the blight caused both by poverty and the Westway has to be recognised.

There is also, despite all efforts to diminish it, much tension in the area. Just as the old landlords feared the ghettos of poverty which surrounded their neighbourhoods, so those in the gentrified areas of Ladbroke, Pembridge and Chepstow feel uncomfortably close to this drabness. It may be tidier, certainly more spacious and sanitary than what it replaced, but it still teeters on the edge of squalor, and so much of it is undeniably ugly and barren. There is also the racial tension which surfaces every now and again, not just between black and white, but between various ethnic groups.

Certainly the affair of the Mangrove Restaurant has done nothing to reduce tension. In All Saints Road, which was once to lead to poor clergyman Walker's 'cathedral', the Mangrove, a restaurant run by Frank Critchlow, a father-figure in the West Indian community, had established itself as a black centre. It is alleged that on many occasions the police picked on the Mangrove, raiding it without good reason in search of drugs. Critchlow in 1992 received compensation of £50,000 from the police following allegations of false imprisonment, assault and malicious prosecution, but this will not appease those who think that the police are not even-handed in their relationships with the black community, nor will it cut much ice with those in the Pembridges and the Chepstows who feel threatened by the drug culture and the attendant crime that undoubtedly exists in this part of Notting Hill.

Drugs are only one part of the social problems of the area. Significant and noticeable is that many of the younger generation of the ethnic minorities, jobless and without meaningful participation in the society in which they find themselves, appear to have abandoned the religious and social values of their parents so that they are as different from their inherited cultures as they are from those of the indigenous whites.

There will probably never be a comprehensive solution to the problems and dangers inherent in the situation - no other city has yet resolved similar difficulties. But the fragile peace must be maintained and this can only be done by small-scale endeavours and by very committed people. It would be a tragedy, and an expensive one, if the the local authority was anything but whole-hearted in its support.